MIS with Practical Aspects

Author

Dr. Amit Kumar Gupta

Published By

MIS with Practical Aspects

ISBN 978-93-83459-30-8

Author

Dr. Amit Kumar Gupta
Associate Professor, Shri Ram Institute of Technology
Department of Management, Affiliated to RDVV ,
Jabalpur-MP

Published by

Bonfring
292/2, 5th Street Extension, Gandhipuram,
Coimbatore-641 012. Tamilnadu, India.
E-mail: info@bonfring.org
Website: www.bonfring.org
Contact: 0422 3928700

ABOUT AUTHOR

Dr. Amit Kumar Gupta (b. 1979) obtained his MBA (DAVV, Indore). and Ph.D. degree in Management from Dr. R.M.L. Awadh University Fazabad . He has been teaching Management Discipline and Entrepreneurship skills development at the Postgraduate level at Shri Ram Institute of Technology ,Department of Management, Jabalpur since 2012. He has also worked more in corporate industries in telecommunication .He has presented a number of papers on management and entrepreneurship issues at various National and International Seminars/Journal and Conferences.

He is an active member of the different bodies of Management.

Dr. Amit Kumar Gupta

Associate Professor

Shri Ram Institute of Technology

Department of Management

Affiliated to RDVV, Jabalpur-MP

Acknowledgement

I am overwhelmed with joy, and avail this opportunity, to express my deepest gratitude and sincere regards to people who in one way or the other have helped me throughout the year 2012 to complete my work successfully. The present work would not have come into existence without their altruistic contributions and efforts.

The advice and encouragement I constantly receive from Prof. R.N. Rai for all the Academic endeavours . I undertake cannot be properly expressed in the few sentences I am able to write here.

It gives me immense pleasure to express my deep sense of gratitude to my wife, for her timely advice and perennial encouragement throughout the course of my work.

I also deeply acknowledge the unflinching support, motivation and constant encouragement of my parents whose inspiration constantly helped me a lot in finalizing this project.

Dr. Amit Kumar Gupta

Associate Professor

Shri Ram Institute of Technology

Department of Management

Affiliated to RDVV, Jabalpur-MP

PREFACE

No invention in recent years has had a greater impact on society than the computer. It has changed the way we live our lives, and it has dramatically changed the way we do business. We can collect, process, store, retrieve and distribute information faster than ever before...all with the push of a button. Fossils (from Latin fossils, literally, "obtained by digging") are the preserved remains, impression, or traces of animals or plants of the past.

The basic idea in this book is to "dig-up," expose, and utilize past conceptions, theories, ideas, and uses of Management Information Systems, which have been "fossilized," yet retain a useful structure and utility, and will observe and analyze current trends in Management Information Systems, in order to provide an integrative framework of concepts, methodologies, and infrastructures for an emerging service-based world that will be based on existing and forthcoming advanced technologies.

To create a dynamic environment that mirrors the breadth and depth of our world economy, we seek diversity.

Before the concept of management information systems was created, computer scientists were just programmers creating applications for science and math calculations. As computer usage evolved in fields of business and data management, software applications were needed to process non-scientific data . A field of study would be needed to bridge the gap between computer programmers and the business world to create information-based applications for business and networks.

Management Information Systems is considered as a rather obsolete term – it dates back to the times of centralized computing, mainframes, batch processing, and a report-centric culture in the corporate world.

We talk about information systems that are facilitating management at all levels, hence the term Management Information Systems is still satisfying and reflecting the reality we face today.

MIS revolution is at its height in some advanced countries of the west and east. We must make 21st century as a century of achievements. While a lot has to be done to achieve our goal MIS revolution constitutes one of the most important planks on which we can cross the watershed.

MIS provides an understanding of how information systems and technology can be used effectively by organization,

MIS provide the conceptual and methodological foundations that reflect interdisciplinary concerns regarding research in management information systems. This book investigates the future of management information systems by means of analyzing a variety of MIS and service-related concepts in a wide range of disciplines, including computer science, software engineering, operations research, management of information systems, economics, management theory, marketing, business strategy, as well as novel concepts and knowledge from related areas.

This book attempts to place before the reader all possible and relative terms, theories, concepts and personalities associated with the subjects.

I am confident that this book would be well accepted across a wide spectrum of readers.

Suggestions for further improvement are most welcome and shall be gratefully acknowledged.

Unit I

PRACTICAL ASPECT OF MIS

Many graduates of computer science, computer engineering, information technology and information systems courses start their careers as developers, software engineers or in technical area like network support. However, as their careers develop, they find themselves increasingly confronted with business and management problems which, notwithstanding their technical skills and experience, they have not been trained to handle.

MIS is designed to fill this gap by providing a practical grounding in critical aspects of IS/ICT management together with an understanding of current thinking about ICT management and governance. MIS designed for information systems/technology professionals in early or mid career who:

- have recently been appointed to management positions or
- see their long term career in ICT management or
- would like to understand key business aspects of ICT better or
- are interested in current thinking and research about ICT management.

The demand for MIS skills has seen a tremendous resurgence in the past few years. Forecasts are extremely strong with MIS skill sets dominating the top job roles expected to grow in the future. While the MIS careers are expected to expand at an accelerated rate, the mix of skill requirements has changed considerably. With the explosive growth of technology accompanying the usage of the Internet in the late 1990s, the role of application development (programming) dominated the MIS

1

field. Since then, outsourcing has moved many of the low level programming jobs overseas. However, the increased need for higher level technology jobs has become prevalent. Now, the web, communication and database technologies are maturing and their usage has begun to extend throughout every area of business practices. These new information technologies are being employed in expansive and creative ways. The result is that the need for MIS professionals has increased -- but in a different way than decades past. MIS is now a "people skill" rather than a purely "technical skill". Our MIS program now trains "business analysts" rather than "programmers".

The "business analyst" (or "systems analyst" or "consultant") position has become critical in order to make information technology available to more users and solve more business problems. This requires skills in identifying user and consumer problems and translating these needs into technology solutions. The analyst provides this critical connection. This role is not subject to outsourcing because the analyst must be embedded in the organization in order to understand the business user and their needs and be able to design and implement the solution within the confines of the organization's technology infrastructure. After the entry-level analyst role, most MS professionals become "project managers" (or "senior consultants") where they assume the responsibility for an entire technology project's: planning; staffing; budgeting; implementation scheduling; training and operational maintenance. After this project management level, the MIS professional will transition into senior technology management roles that involve: technology planning and strategy; technology architectures and infrastructures; corporate wide technology staffing; and the management of various critical technology centers. Finally, at the "C" level, the Chief Information Officer (CIO) represents the pinnacle technology role within most corporate environments.

1.1 MANAGEMENT, INFORMATION SYSTEMS AND DIGITAL INNOVATION

The MSc Information Systems and Digital Innovation (MISDI) studies digital innovation in business and government across the world. The internet and mobile technologies are changing the way we create and share information and open opportunities for new business models, new forms of governance, and new ways for public engagement. This prepares students for leadership roles in the shaping of digital innovation and in the management of the business and social transformation that such innovation unleashes.

It is an intellectually rigorous, qualitative, inter-disciplinary programme that integrates established knowledge of the development and management of information systems with the critical study of emerging domains of digital innovation, such as cloud computing, social networking, and big data.

It involves research-led, practice relevant teaching. Our learning approach requires critical essay writing as we place emphasis on theory and critical discussion of academic literature from across a range of scientific fields. We include social theories and frameworks for understanding the processes of information systems and innovation and case studies for illustrating issues in particular instances of management and innovation practice.

1.2 INFORMATION SYSTEMS

Information system (IS) is the study of complementary networks of hardware and software that people and organizations use to collect, filter, process, create, and distribute data.

The study bridges business and computer science using the theoretical foundations of information and computation to study various business models and related algorithmic processes within a computer science discipline.

Computer information system(s) (CIS) is a field studying computers and algorithmic processes, including their principles, their software and hardware designs, their applications, and their impact on society while IS emphasizes functionality over design.

Any specific information system aims to support operations, management and decision making. In a broad sense, the term is used to refer not only to the information and communication technology (ICT) that an organization uses, but also to the way in which people interact with this technology in support of business processes.

Some authors make a clear distinction between information systems, computer systems, and business processes. Information systems typically include an ICT component but are not purely concerned with ICT, focusing instead on the end use of information technology. Information systems are also different from business processes.

Information systems help to control the performance of business processes.

Alter argues for advantages of viewing an information system as a special type of work system. A work system is a system in which humans and/or machines perform work (processes and activities) using resources to produce specific products and/or services for customers. An information system is a work system whose activities are devoted to processing (capturing, transmitting, storing, retrieving, manipulating and displaying) information.

As such, information systems inter-relate with data systems on the one hand and activity systems on the other. An information system is a form of communication system in which data represent and are processed as a form of social memory. An information system can also be considered a semi-formal language which supports human decision making and action.

Information systems are the primary focus of study for organizational informatics.[

1.3 HISTORY

CS, SE, IS, IT, & Customer Venn Diagramwhere functionality spans left and design spans right stemming from discovery.

The history of systems coincides with the history of computer science that began long before the modern discipline of computer science emerged in the twentieth century. Regarding the circulation of information and ideas, numerous legacy information systems still exist today that are continuously updated to promote ethnographic approaches, to ensure data integrity, and to improve the social effectiveness & efficiency of the whole process.In general, information systems are focused upon processing information within organizations, especially within business enterprises, and sharing the benefits with modern society.

1.4 OVERVIEW

Silver et al. (1995) provided two views on IS that includes software, hardware, data, people, and procedures. Zheng provided another system view of information system which also adds processes and essential system elements like environment, boundary, purpose, and interactions. The Association for Computing Machinery defines "Information systems specialists [as] focus[ing] on integrating information technology solutions and business processes to meet the information needs of businesses and other enterprises.

There are various types of information systems, for example: transaction processing systems, decision support systems, knowledge management systems, learning management systems, database management systems, and office information systems. Critical to most information systems are information technologies, which are typically designed to enable humans to perform tasks for which the human brain is not well suited, such as: handling large amounts of information, performing complex calculations, and controlling many simultaneous processes.

Information technologies are a very important and malleable resource available to executives.[30] Many companies have created a position of

Chief Information Officer (CIO) that sits on the executive board with the Chief Executive Officer (CEO), Chief Financial Officer (CFO), Chief Operating Officer (COO) and Chief Technical Officer (CTO). The CTO may also serve as CIO [Chief Information Officer], and vice versa. The Chief Information Security Officer (CISO) focuses on information security management.

1.5 THE DISCIPLINE OF INFORMATION SYSTEMS

Several IS scholars have debated the nature and foundations of Information Systems which has its roots in other reference disciplines such as Computer Science, Engineering, Mathematics, Management Science, Cybernetics, and others.[31][32][33][34] Information systems also can be defined as a collection of hardware, software, data, people and procedures that work together to produce quality information.

The impact on economic models

- Microeconomic theory model
- Transaction cost theory
- Agency theory

DIFFERENTIATING IS FROM RELATED DISCIPLINES

Information Systems relationship toInformation Technology, Computer Science,Information Science, and Business.

Similar to computer science, other disciplines can be seen as both related and foundation disciplines of IS. The domain of study of IS involves the study of theories and practices related to the social and technological phenomena, which determine the development, use, and effects of information systems in organization and society. But, while there may be considerable overlap of the disciplines at the boundaries, the disciplines are still differentiated by the focus, purpose, and orientation of their activities.

In a broad scope, the term Information Systems is a scientific field of study that addresses the range of strategic, managerial, and operational activities involved in the gathering, processing, storing, distributing, and use of information and its associated technologies in society and organizations.The term information systems is also used to describe an organizational function that applies IS knowledge in industry, government agencies, and not-for-profit organizations. Information Systems often refers to the interaction between algorithmic processes and technology. This interaction can occur within or across organizational boundaries. An information system is the technology an organization uses and also the way in which the organizations interact with the technology and the way in which the technology works with the organization's business processes. Information systems are distinct from information technology (IT) in that an information system has an information technology component that interacts with the processes' components.

TYPES OF INFORMATION SYSTEMS

A four level pyramid model of different types of Information Systems based on the different levels of hierarchy in an organization

The "classic" view of Information systems found in the textbooks in the 1980s was of a pyramid of systems that reflected the hierarchy of the organization, usually transaction processing systems at the bottom of the pyramid, followed by management information systems, decision support systems, and ending with executive information systems at the top. Although the pyramid model remains useful, since it was first formulated a number of new technologies have been developed and new categories of information systems have emerged, some of which no longer fit easily into the original pyramid model.

Some examples of such systems are:

- data warehouses
- enterprise resource planning
- enterprise systems
- expert systems
- search engines
- geographic information system
- global information system
- office automation.

A Computer(-Based) Information System is essentially an IS using computer technology to carry out some or all of its planned tasks. The basic components of computer based information system are:

- **Hardware-** these are the devices like the monitor, processor, printer and keyboard, all of which work together to accept, process, show data and information.
- **Software-** are the programs that allow the hardware to process the data.
- **Databases-** are the gathering of associated files or tables containing related data.

- **Networks-** are a connecting system that allows diverse computers to distribute resources.

- **Procedures-** are the commands for combining the components above to process information and produce the preferred output.

The first four components (hardware, software, database and network) make up what is known as the information technology platform. Information technology workers could then use these components to create information systems that watch over safety measures, risk and the management of data. These actions are known as information technology services.

Certain information systems support parts of organizations, others support entire organizations, and still others, support groups of organizations. Recall that each department or functional area within an organization has its own collection of application programs, or information systems. These functional area information systems (FAIS) are supporting pillars for more general IS namely, business intelligencesystems and dashboards. As the name suggest, each FAIS support a particular function are within the organization, e.g.: accounting IS, finance IS, production/operation management (POM) IS, marketing IS, and human resources IS. In finance and accounting, managers use IT systems to forecast revenues and business activity, to determine the best sources and uses of funds, and to perform audits to ensure that the organization is fundamentally sound and that all financial reports and documents are accurate. Other types of organizational information systems are FAIS, Transaction processing systems,enterprise resource planning, office automation system, management information system, decision support system, expert system, executive dashboard, supply chain management system, and electronic commerce system. Dashboards are a special form of IS that support all managers of the organization. They provide rapid access to timely information and direct access to structured information in the form of reports. Expert systems attempt to duplicate the work of human experts by applying reasoning capabilities, knowledge, and expertise within a specific domain.

Information systems career pathways

Information Systems have a number of different areas of work:

- IS strategy
- IS management
- IS development
- IS iteration
- IS organization

There is a wide variety of career paths in the information systems discipline. "Workers with specialized technical knowledge and strong communications skills will have the best prospects. Workers with management skills and an understanding of business practices and principles will have excellent opportunities, as companies are increasingly looking to technology to drive their revenue.

INFORMATION SYSTEMS DEVELOPMENT

Information technology departments in larger organizations tend to strongly influence information technology development, use, and application in the organizations, which may be a business or corporation. A series of methodologies and processes can be used to develop and use an information system. Many developers have turned and used a more engineering approach such as the System Development Life Cycle (SDLC) which is a systematic procedure of developing an information system through stages that occur in sequence. An Information system can be developed in house (within the organization) or outsourced. This can be accomplished by outsourcing certain components or the entire system.. A specific case is the geographical distribution of the development team (Offshoring, Global Information System).

A computer based information system, following a definition of **Langefors,**

- a technologically implemented medium for recording, storing, and disseminating linguistic expressions,
- as well as for drawing conclusions from such expressions.

which can be formulated as a generalized information systems design mathematical program.

Geographic Information Systems, Land Information systems and Disaster Information Systems are also some of the emerging information systems but they can be broadly considered as Spatial Information Systems. System development is done in stages which include:

- Problem recognition and specification
- Information gathering
- Requirements specification for the new system

- System design

- System construction

- System implementation

- Review and maintenance.

INFORMATION SYSTEMS RESEARCH

Information systems research is generally interdisciplinary concerned with the study of the effects of information systems on the behavior of individuals, groups, and organizations Hevner et al. (2004) categorized research in IS into two scientific paradigms including behavioral science which is to develop and verify theories that explain or predict human or organizational behavior and design science which extends the boundaries of human and organizational capabilities by creating new and innovative artifacts.

Salvatore March and Gerald Smith proposed a framework for researching different aspects of Information Technology including outputs of the research (research outputs) and activities to carry out this research (research activities). They identified research outputs as follows:

1. Constructs which are concepts that form the vocabulary of a domain. They constitute a conceptualization used to describe problems within the domain and to specify their solutions.

2. A model which is a set of propositions or statements expressing relationships among constructs.

3. A method which is a set of steps (an algorithm or guideline) used to perform a task. Methods are based on a set of underlying constructs and a representation (model) of the solution space.

4. An instantiation is the realization of an artifact in its environment.

Also research activities including:

1. Build an artifact to perform a specific task.

2. Evaluate the artifact to determine if any progress has been achieved.

3. Given an artifact whose performance has been evaluated, it is important to determine why and how the artifact worked or did not work within its environment. Therefore theorize and justify theories about IT artifacts.

Although Information Systems as a discipline has been evolving for over 30 years now the core focus or identity of IS research is still subject to debate among scholars.There are two main views around this debate: a narrow view focusing on the IT artifact as the core subject matter of IS research, and a broad view that focuses on the interplay between social and technical aspects of IT that is embedded into a dynamic evolving context. A third view calls on IS scholars to pay balanced attention to both the IT artifact and its context.

Since the study of information systems is an applied field, industry practitioners expect information systems research to generate findings that are immediately applicable in practice. This is not always the case however, as information systems researchers often explore behavioral issues in much more depth than practitioners would expect them to do.

This may render information systems research results difficult to understand, and has led to criticism.

To study an information system itself, rather than its effects, information systems models are used, such as EATPUT.

The international body of Information Systems researchers, the Association for Information Systems (AIS), and its Senior Scholars Forum Subcommittee on Journals (23 April 2007), proposed a 'basket' of journals that the AIS deems as 'excellent', and nominated: Management Information Systems Quarterly (MISQ), Information Systems Research (ISR), Journal of the Association for Information Systems (JAIS),Journal of Management Information Systems (JMIS), European Journal of Information Systems (EJIS), and Information Systems Journal (ISJ).

A number of annual information systems conferences are run in various parts of the world, the majority of which are peer reviewed. The AIS directly runs the International Conference on Information Systems(ICIS) and the Americas Conference on Information Systems (AMCIS), while AIS affiliated conferences include the Pacific Asia Conference on Information Systems (PACIS), European Conference on Information Systems (ECIS), the Mediterranean Conference on Information Systems (MCIS), the International Conference on Information Resources Management (Conf-IRM) and the Wuhan International Conference on E-Business (WHICEB). AIS chapter conferences include Australasian Conference on Information Systems (ACIS), Information Systems Research Conference in Scandinavia

(IRIS), Conference of the Italian Chapter of AIS (itAIS), Annual Mid-Western AIS Conference (MWAIS) and Annual Conference of the Southern AIS (SAIS).

COMPONENTS

The 5 components that must come together in order to produce a Computer-Based Information system are:

1. **Hardware:**The term hardware refers to machinery.This category includes the computer itself, which is often referred to as the central processing unit (CPU), and all of its support equipments. Among the support equipments are input and output devices, storage devices and communications devices.

2. **Software:**The term software refers to computer programs and the manuals (if any) that support them. Computer programs are machine-readable instructions that direct the circuitry within the hardware parts of the system to function in ways that produce useful information from data. Programs are generally stored on some input / output medium,often a disk or tape.

3. **Data:**Data are facts that are used by programs to produce useful information.Like programs,data are generally stored in machine-readable form on disk or tape until the computer needs them.

4. **Procedures**:Procedures are the policies that govern the operation of a computer system. "Procedures are to people what software is to hardware" is a common analogy that is used to illustrate the role of procedures in a system.

5. **People**:Every system needs people if it is to be useful. Often the most over-looked element of the system are the people, probably the component that most influence the success or failure of information systems.

SERVICE ECONOMY

Over the past two decades, the service economy has become the largest part of most industrialized nations' economies according to key economic indices, such as contribution to GDP and employment. In parallel, the concept of service has been developed in different disciplines as a key theoretical construct that drastically impacts recent research initiatives.

Management Information Systems for Enterprise Applications: Business Issues, Research and Solutions provide the conceptual and methodological foundations that reflect interdisciplinary concerns regarding research in management information systems. This book investigates the future of management information systems by means of analyzing a variety of MIS and service-related concepts in a wide range of disciplines, including computer science, software engineering, operations research, management of information systems, economics, management theory, marketing, business strategy, cognitive sciences, anthropology, humanities and the arts, as well as novel concepts and knowledge from related areas.

Unit II

Management Information System

2.1 Introduction to Management Information Systems

MIS (Management Information Systems)

- E-Mail
- Print
- A
- AA
- AAA
- inshore
- Face book
- Twitter
- Share This
- RSS
- Reprints

MIS (management information systems) is a general term for the computer systems in an enterprise that provide information about its business operations. It's also used to refer to the people who manage these systems. Typically, in a large corporation, "MIS" or the "MIS department" refers to a central or centrally-coordinated system of computer expertise and management, often including mainframe systems but also including by extension the corporation's entire network of computer resources.

In the beginning, business computers were used for the practical business of computing the payroll and keeping track of accounts payable and receivable. As applications were developed that provided managers with information about sales, inventories, and other data that would help in managing the enterprise, the term "MIS" arose to describe these kinds of applications. Today, the term is used broadly in a number of contexts and includes (but is not limited to): decision support systems, resource and people management applications, project management, and database retrieval applications.

Margaret Rouse

A **management information system** (**MIS**) provides information that organizations require to manage themselves efficiently and effective Management information systems are typically computer systems used for managing. The five primary components: 1.) *Hardware,* 2.) *Software,* 3.) *Data* (*information for decision making),* 4.) Procedures (design,development and documentation), and 5.) People (individuals, groups, or organizations). Management information systems are distinct from other information systems because they are used to analyze and facilitate strategic and operational activities.

Academically, the term is commonly used to refer to the study of how individuals, groups, and organizations evaluate, design, implement, manage, and utilize systems to generate information to improve efficiency and effectiveness of decision making, including systems termed decision support systems, expert systems, and executive information systems Most business schools (or colleges of business administration within universities) have an MIS department, alongside departments of accounting, finance, management, marketing, and sometimes others, and grant degrees (at undergrad, masters, and PhD levels) in MIS.

A MIS gives business managers the information they need to make decisions and solve problems, while facilitating data from different aspects of a project

Early business computers were used for simple operations such as tracking inventory, billing, sales, or payroll data, with little detail or structuree EDP. Over time, these computer applications became more complex and previously isolated applications, such as card systems and magnetic storage, became connected in the 1980s and allowed a way to network the information together. With greater computing capability and the networks to link the necessary information, MIS became a standard among many companies.

Originally, MIS described applications providing managers with information about sales, inventories, and other data that would help in managing the enterprise. Over time, the term broadened to include:decision support systems, resource management and human resource management, enterprise resource planning, enterprise performance management, supply chain management, customer relationship management, project management and database retrieval applications.

An MIS provides three types of information to managers:

- Detailed, which confirms activities
- Summary, which puts information in an easy-to-read form

- Exception, which deals with all information outside the normal scope of activities

Kenneth C. Laudon and Jane Laudon identify five *eras* of MIS evolution corresponding to the five phases in the development of computing technology:

1) mainframe and minicomputer computing

2) personal computers

3) client/server networks

4) Enterprise computing

5) Cloud computing.

2.2 BACKGROUND

The *first era* (mainframe and minicomputer) was ruled by IBM and their mainframe computers; these computers would often take up whole rooms and require teams to run them - IBM supplied the hardware and the software. As technology advanced, these computers were able to handle greater capacities and therefore reduce their cost. Smaller, more affordable minicomputers allowed larger businesses to run their own computing centers in-house.

The *second era* (personal computer) began in 1965 as microprocessors started to compete with mainframes and minicomputers and accelerated the process of decentralizing computing power from large data centers to smaller offices. In the late 1970s minicomputer technology gave way to personal computers and relatively low cost computers were becoming mass market commodities, allowing businesses to provide their employees access to computing power that ten years before would have cost tens of thousands of dollars. This proliferation of computers created a ready market for interconnecting networks and the popularization of the Internet.

As technological complexity increased and costs decreased, the need to share information within an enterprise also grew—giving rise to the *third era* (client/server), in which computers on a common network access shared information on a server. This lets thousands and even millions of people access data simultaneously. The *fourth era* (enterprise) enabled by high speed networks, tied all aspects of the business enterprise together offering rich information access encompassing the complete management structure. Every computer is utilized.

The *fifth era* (cloud computing) is the latest and employs networking technology to deliver applications as well as data storage independent of the configuration, location or nature of the hardware. This, along with high speed cellphone and wifi networks, led to new levels of mobility in which managers access the MIS remotely with laptop and tablet computers, plus smartphones.

2.3 TYPES AND TERMINOLOGY

The terms *Management Information System* (MIS), *information system*, *Enterprise Resource Planning* (ERP), and *information technology management* are often confused. Information systems and MIS are broader categories that include ERP. Information technology management concerns the operation and organization of information technology resources independent of their purpose.

Most management information systems specialize in particular commercial and industrial sectors, aspects of the enterprise, or management substructure.

- *Management information systems*, produce fixed, regularly scheduled reports based on data extracted and summarized from the firm's underlying transaction processing systemsto middle and operational level managers to identify and inform structured and semi-structured decision problems.

- *Decision Support Systems (DSS)* are computer program applications used by middle and higher management to compile information from a wide range of sources to support problem solving and decision making.DSS is majorly used for semi-structured and unstructured decision problems.

- *Executive Information Systems (EIS)* is a reporting tool that provides quick access to summarized reports coming from all company levels and departments such as accounting, human resources and operations.

- *Marketing Information Systems* are Management Information Systems designed specifically for managing the marketing aspects of the business.

- *Office Automation Systems (OAS)* support communication and productivity in the enterprise by automating work flow and eliminating bottlenecks. OAS may be implemented at any and all levels of management.

- *School Information Management Systems* (SIMS) cover school administration,and often including teaching and learning materials.
- *Enterprise Resource Planning* facilitates the flow of information between all business functions inside the boundaries of the organization and manage the connections to outside stakeholders.

2.4 ADVANTAGES

The following are some of the benefits that can be attained for different types of MISs.

- Companies are able to highlight their strengths and weaknesses due to the presence of revenue reports, employees' performance record etc. The identification of these aspects can help the company improve their business processes and operations.
- Giving an overall picture of the company and acting as a communication and planning tool.
- The availability of customer data and feedback can help the company to align their business processes according to the needs of the customers. The effective management of customer data can help the company to perform direct marketing and promotion activities.
- MISs can help a company gain a competitive advantage. Competitive advantage is a firm's ability to do something better,

faster, cheaper, or uniquely, when compared with rival firms in the market.

ENTERPRISE APPLICATIONS

- *Enterprise systems*—also known as *enterprise resource planning (ERP)* systems—provide integrated software modules and a unified database that personnel use to plan, manage, and control core business processes across multiple locations. Modules of ERP systems may include finance, accounting, marketing, human resources, production, inventory management, and distribution.

- *Supply chain management (SCM)* systems enable more efficient management of the supply chain by integrating the links in a supply chain. This may include suppliers, manufacturers, wholesalers, retailers, and final customers.

- *Customer relationship management (CRM)* systems help businesses manage relationships with potential and current customers and business partners across marketing, sales, and service.

- *Knowledge management system (KMS)* helps organizations facilitate the collection, recording, organization, retrieval, and dissemination of knowledge. This may include documents, accounting records, unrecorded procedures, practices, and skills. Knowledge management (KM) as a system covers the process of knowledge creation and acquisition from internal processes and the external world. The collected knowledge is incorporated in organizational policies and procedures, and then disseminated to the stakeholders.

- Developing Information Systems

The actions that are taken to create an information system that solves an organizational problem are called system development.These include system analysis, system design, computer programming/implementation, testing, conversion, production and finally maintenance. These actions usually take place in that specified order but some may need to repeat or be accomplished concurrently.

Conversion is the process of changing or converting the old system into the new. This can be done in three basic ways, though newer methods (prototyping, Extreme Programming, JAD, etc.) are replacing these traditional conversion methods in many cases:

- Direct cut – The new system replaces the old at an appointed time.
- Pilot study — Introducing the new system to a small portion of the operation to see how it fares. If good then the new system expands to the rest of the company.
- Phased approach – New system is introduced in stages.

2.5 COMMUNICATION TECHNOLOGY

MANAGEMENT INFORMATION SYSTEM, FUNCTIONS, STRUCTURE AND ITS IMPORTANCE IN MANAGER'S DECISION MAKING

Management Information Systems can be used in various forms in organizations and businesses. Some cases such as activities, problem solving, organizational and follow up business opportunities with using it will be possible. Management Information Systems is a useful tool that provided organized and summarized information in a proper time to decision makers and Enable making accurate decision for managers in organizations or in other words, it's a system that receives data from different units and produce information and provide Timely and accurate information for different levels of managers for making optimal decision. In this paper we intend to evaluate the components of (MIS) and the role of it in making decision process.

MANAGEMENT INFORMATION SYSTEM (MIS) CONCEPT

Most important issues in managing an organization's are decision making."**Peter Drucker"** believes that future management; focus on decision-making process and understanding. Therefore many management experts believe that decision making synonymous is management, or it's the most important part of it. Considering that make decisions without necessary information is not available, Basis for such a task is to providing necessary information for management. In the today Complex modern world, the role of Management Information Systems and its inevitable impact on society and organizations is not hiding from anyone. Lack of ensuring what's happening to the future and Lack of information on current events forced the manager go formal or informal information communication. Information is the cultured data in the organization that through order of their communication to provide accurate information, increases ensure managing in making decisions. A rapid change of outside organization factors has increased the need of manager for organization development and complexity of management systems. Damage that caused by poor decisions are Irreparable. The impact of timely and good strategic decisions cannot be described. But the noticeable point is that providing timely information, accurate, convenient and brief and communication at all levels of organizational management requires efficient information management system to facilitate right decisions and planning and control administrative duties for management. Obviously decision making in efficient and effective manner, especially in today's complex and evolving world requires the use of very large amounts of information. In fact, information is an important strategic tool in decision making management, And without a doubt quality of management decisions related to the accuracy of the information that is provided at the time of making decision. The extent of changes in domestic and foreign organizations and communities, gradually reveal the need for making complex decisions for managers. So that today without access to, it's not possible to decision making into scientific concept. **"Dunken"** Knows one of the most striking features of the transition from simple to complex environments static or dynamic environments uncertainty and unpredictable action and unplanned decisions. Information Systems(IS) has an important and key role in organizations of third Millennium. Nowadays, an information system has excellent effect on the structure of organizational hierarchy. Therefore, considering to conditions governing organizations and communities, manager should understand importance of information or access to it, particularly in relation to unplanned decisions and reduce of uncertainty. By using decision support systems (DSS),and try in order to obtain detailed information, accurate and timely decision-making as an essential and valuable resource and asset. Thus, in this paper, has been investigated the importance of making decision and role of in organizations to improving the quality of this crucial process.

BACKGROUND OF STUDY

Knowledge of MIS, which is one branch of information science, or more precisely, is one of Systems science, has a history less than forty-year. Although this new scientific paradigm has experienced significant changes, But compared with its related sciences like information technology and communication,intelligence and cognitive science, is still has a long way with a lot of up and down. The concept of MIS, which was formed in 1965 in the United States, quickly influence most academic center of word and especially in the departments of management and became popular. Can be said, this trend passed almost two-thirds of its evolution until 1995.Many researchers and scientists of information science provide important Studies and researches about development of MIS and each of them looked from a different point of view have been published some analyzes. A new attitude that is coming soon shows that the demands of a dynamic economy requires a new style of decision making and new approaches in organizations And this coordination, induced production and dissemination of information in present time that force Organizations to review their activities. The new period that known as informatics age, promise a new world with new ways of using information. Information technology that was as a competitive advantage and a strategic weapon year ago, today it is considered as a competitive need. New information and communication technology as a pervasive wave changes in all aspects of human life, including in the field of management and Mass media, telecommunications, information systems and… have changed the way of doing things. Today, considering the cost of information technology and the other hand the inevitability of using it, it is necessary to know the steps taken in this way and the managers should aware of the effects of it individuals, work groups and organizations. Therefore, in this paper investigate way of working decision making process at the level of organization's manager.

1. *Definition of system:* System is a set of interconnected components that follow specific goals. There are two types of systems, each system has two settings: A) Outer perimeter: an area that the manager can not have much control over it B) The internal perimeter is an area that manager can have much control over it.

2. *Definition of data* The facts are achieved by observation and research and recorded called data. Data is often called raw information. The point is that the data can be obtained from local sources.

3. *Definition of information* Data, after processing convert to information if it has any meaning. Information, actually data are transformed data that provide a particular meaning .

4. *Characteristics of the appropriate information*: There are four characteristics of useful information: • Timeliness: the timeliness

refers to whether during decision-making it is possible to access the information or not. • Quality: Quality means the accuracy of the information. People can easily take the wrong decisions, with wrong information. • Completeness: completeness, indicate to the amount of data collected, And relevancy refer to the amount of data communication with objectives of the decision. • Relevancy: appropriate criteria and information will help managers to choose the correct option

5. *General purpose of information* In a general view, provide the information needed to make decisions. This work will be done via describes the condition of phenomena, explaining events, predicting events, proposed solutions, and eventually evaluate present activities.

6. *Definition of management:* There is no consensus on the definition of management and Scholars and theorists of management knowledge with different biases and goals have been proposed different definitions. • Management is the art of doing work by others. Process of converting information into action, the process of change and conversion called decision making . • Process of synchronization group and individual activities in order to group's . Process of planning, organizing, leading , controlling work of organizational members and using all available resources to achieve desired goals of organization(Daft & Richard,2012).

7. *Defining Information System:* Information systems are the systems that collect, processing, storing, analyzing and distribute information for a special purpose. Each information system are consists of hardware, software, data, procedures, individuals.

The concept of the MIS has evolved over a period of time comprising many different facets of the organizational function. MIS is a necessity of all the organizations. The initial concept of MIS was to process data from the organization and present it in the for of reports at regular intervals. The system was largely capable of handling the data from collection to processing. It was more impersonal, requiring each individual to pick and choose the processed data and use it for his requirements. This concept was further modified when a distinction was made between data and information. The information is a product of an analysis of data. This concept is similar to a raw material and the finished product. What are needed are information and not a mass of data. However, the data can be analyzed in a number of ways, producing different shades and specifications of the information as a product. It was, therefore, demanded that the system concept be an individual-oriented, as each individual may have a different orientation. Towards the information. This concept was further modified, that the system should present information in such a form and format that it creates an impact on its user, provoking a decision or an investigation. It was later realized then even though such an impact was a welcome modification, some sort of selective approach was necessary in the analysis and reporting. Hence, the concept of exception reporting was imbibed in MIS.

The concept remained valid till and to the extent that the norm for an exception remained true and effective. Since the environment turns competitive and is ever changing, fixation of the norm for an exception becomes ka futile exercise at least for the people in the higher echelons of the organization. The concept was then evolved that the system should be capable of handling a need based exception reporting. This need maybe either of an individual or a group of people. This called for keeping all data together in such a form that it can be accessed by anybody and can be processed to suit his needs. The concept is that the data is one but it can be viewed by different individuals in different ways. This gave rise to the concept of DA .ABASE, and the MIS based on the DATABASE proved much more effective. Over a period of time, when these conceptual developments were taking place, the concept of the end user computing using multiple databases emerged. This concept brought a fundamental charge in MIS. The change was decentralization of the system and the user of the in formation becoming independent of computer professionals. When this becomes a reality, the concept of MIS changed to a decision making system. The job in a computer department is to manage the information resource and leave the task of information processing to the user. The concept of MIS in today.s world is a system which handles the databases, databases, provides com-putting facilities to the end user and gives a variety of decision making tools to the user of the system. The concept of MIS gives high regard to the individual and his ability to use information. An MIS gives information through data analysis. While analyzing the data, it relies on many academic disciplines. These include the theories, principles and concepts from the Management Science, Psychology and Human Behavior, making the MID more effective and useful. These academic disciplines are used in designing the MIS, evolving the decision support tools for modeling and decision - making. The foundation of MIS is the principles of management and if its practices. MIS uses the concept of management Information System can be evolved for a specific objective if it is evolved after systematic planning and design. It calls for an analysis of a business, management views and policies, organization culture and the culture and the management style. The information should be generated in this setting and must be useful in managing the business. This is possible only when it in conceptualized as system with an appropriate design. The MIS, therefore, relies heavily on the systems theory offers solutions to handle the complex situations of the input and output flows. It uses theories of communication which helps to evolve a system design capable of handling data inputs, process, and outputs with the least possible noise or distortion in transmitting the information form a source to a destination. It uses the principles of system Design, Viz., an ability of continuous adjustment or correction in the system in line with the environmental change in which the MIS operates. Such a design help to keep the MIS tuned with the business managements needs of the organization.

The concept, therefore, is a blend of principle, theories and practices of the Management, Information and System giving rise to single product known as Management Information System (MIS). The Physical view of the MIS can be seen as assembly of several subsystems based on the databases in the organization. These subsystems range from data collection, transaction processing and validating, processing, analyzing and storing the information in databases. the subsystem could be at a functional level or a corporate level. The information is evolved through them for a functional or a department management and it provides the information for the management of business at the corporate level. The physical view of the MIS can be shown as in Fig.1.2. The MIS is a product of a multi- disciplinary approach to the business management. It is a product which needs to be kept under a constant review and modification to meet the corporate needs of the information. It is prescribed product design for the organization. The MIS differs since the people in two organizations involved in the same business. The MIS is for the people in the organization. The MIS model may be the same but it differs greatly in the contents.

The MIS, therefore, is a dynamic concept subject to change, time and again, with a change in the business management process. It continuously interacts with the internal and the external environment of the business and provides a corrective mechanism in the system so that the change needs of information are with effectively. The MIS, therefore, is a dynamic design, the primary objectively. The MIS, therefore, is a dynamic design the rimary objective of which is to the information the information for decision making and it is developed considering the organizational fabric, giving due regard to the people in the organizational the management functions and the managerial and the managerial control. The MIS model of the organization changes over a time as the business passes through several phases of developmental growth cycle. It supports the management of the business in each phase by giving the information which is crucial in that phase. Every The MIS model of the organization changes over a time as the business passes through several phases of developmental growth cycle. It supports the management of the business in each phase by giving the information which is crucial in that phase. Every has critical success factors in each phase of growth cycle and the MIS model gives more information on the critical success factors for decision making.

2.6 MIS Definitions

The Management Information System (MIS) is a concept of the last decade or two. It has been understood and described in a number ways. It is also known as the Information System, the Information and Decision System, the Computer- based information System.

The MIS has more than one definition, some of which are give below.

1. The MIS is defined as a system which provides information support for decision making in the organization.

2. The MIS is defined as an integrated system of man and machine for providing the information to support the operations, the management and the decision making function in the organization.

3. The MIS is defined as a system based on the database of the organization evolved for the purpose of providing information to the people in the organization.

4. The MIS is defined as a Computer . based Information System. Thought there are a number of definitions, all of them converge on one single point, i.e., the MIS is a system to support the decision making function in the organization. The difference lies in defining the elements of the MIS. However, in today.s world MIS a computerized .business processing system generating information for the people in the organization to meet the information needs decision making to achieve the corporate objective of the organization.

In any organization, small or big, a major portion of the time goes in data collection, processing, documenting it to the people. Hence, a major portion of the overheads goes into this kind of unproductive work in the organization. Every individual in an organization is continuously looking for some information which is needed to perform his/her task. Hence, the information is people-oriented and it varies with the nature of the people in the organization. The difficulty in handling this multiple requirement of the people is due to a couple of reasons. The information is a processed product to fulfill an imprecise need of the people.

The scope and the quantum of information is individual-dependent and it is difficult to conceive the information as a well-defined product for the entire organization. Since the people are instrumental in any business transaction, a human error is possible in conducting the same. Since a human error is difficult to control, the difficulty arises in ensuring a hundred per cent quality assurance of information in terms of completeness, accuracy, validity, timeliness and meeting the decision making needs. In order to get a better grip on the activity of information processing, it is necessary to have a formal system which should take care of the following points:

- Handling of a voluminous data.
- Confirmation of the validity of data and transaction.
- Complex processing of data and multidimensional analysis.
- Quick search and retrieval.
- Mass storage.
- Communication of the information system to the user on time.
- Fulfilling the changing needs of the information.

The management information system uses computers and communication technology to deal with these points of supreme importance.

2.7 ROLE OF THE MANAGEMENT INFORMATION SYSTEM

The role of the MIS in an organization can be compared to the role of heart in the body. The information is the blood and MIS is the heart. In the body the heart plays the role of supplying pure blood to all the elements of the body including the brain. The heart works faster and supplies more blood when needed. It regulates and controls the incoming impure blood, processes it and sends it to the destination in the quantity needed. It fulfills the needs of blood supply to human body in normal course and also in crisis. The MIS plays exactly the same role in the organization. The system ensures that an appropriate data is collected from the various sources, processed, and sent further to all the needy destinations. The system is expected to fulfill the information needs of an individual, a group of individuals, the management functionaries: the managers and the top management.

The MIS satisfies the diverse needs through a variety of systems such as Query Systems, Analysis Systems, Modeling Systems and Decision Support Systems the MIS helps in Strategic Planning, Management Control, Operational Control and Transaction Processing. The MIS helps the clerical personnel in the transaction processing and answers their queries on the data pertaining to the transaction, the status of a particular record and references on a variety of documents. The MIS helps the junior management personnel by providing the operational data for planning, scheduling and control, and helps them further in decision making at the operations level to correct an out of control situation. The MIS helps the middle management in short them planning, target setting and controlling the business functions. It is supported by the use of the management tools of planning and control. The MIS helps the top management in goal setting, strategic planning and evolving the business plans and their implementation. The MIS plays the role of information generation, communication, problem identification and helps in the process of decision making. The MIS, therefore, plays a vital role in the management, administration and operations of an organization.

IMPACT OF THE MANAGEMENT INFORMATION SYSTEM

Since the MIS plays a very important role in the organization, it creates an impact on the organization.s functions, performance and productivity. The impact of MIS on the functions is in its management. With a good support, the management of marking, finance, production and personnel become more efficient. The tracking and monitoring of the functional targets becomes easy. The functional, managers are informed about the progress, achievements and shortfalls in the probable trends in the various aspects of business. This helps in forecasting and long- term perspective planning. The manager.s attention is brought to a situation which is exceptional in nature, inducing him to take an action or a decision in the matter. A disciplined information reporting system creates a structured data and a knowledge base for all the people in the organization. The information is available in such a form that it can be used straight away or by blending analysis, saving the manager's valuable time.

The MIS creates another impact in the organization which relates to the understanding of the business itself. The MIS begins with the definition of a data entity and its attributes. It uses a dictionary if data, entity and attributes, respectively, designed for information generation in the organization. Since all the information system use the dictionary, there is common understanding of terms and terminology in the organization brining clarity in the communication and a similar understanding an even of the organization. The MIS calls for a systemization of the business operation for an affective system design. A well designed system with a focus on the manger makes an impact on the managerial efficiency. The fund of information motivates an enlightened manger to use a variety of tools of the management. It helps him to resort to such exercises as experimentation and modeling. The use of computers enables him to use the tools techniques which are impossible to use manually. The ready-made packages make this task simpler. The impact is on the managerial ability to perform. It improves the decision making ability considerably. Since the MIS works on the basic systems such as transaction processing and databases, the drudgery of the clerical work is transferred to the computerized system, relieving the human mind for better work. It will be observed that a lot of manpower is engaged in this activity in the organization. It you study the individuals time utilization and its application; you will find that seventy per cent of the time is spent in recording, searching, processing and communication. This is a large overhead in the organization. The MIS has a direct impact on this overhead. It creates an information-based work culture in the organization.

MANAGEMENT INFORMATION SYSTEM AND COMPUTER

Translating the real concept of the MIS into reality is technically, an infeasible proposition unless computers are used. The MIS relies heavily on the hardware and software capacity of the computer and its ability to process, retrieve communicate with no serious limitations. The variety of the hardware having distinct capabilities makes it possible to design the MIS for a specific situation. For example, if the organization needs a large database and very little processing, a computer system is available for such a requirement. Suppose the organization has multiple business location at long distances and if the need is to bring the data at one place, process, and then send the information to various location, it is possible to have a computer system with a distributed data processing capability. If the distance is too long, then the computer system can be hooked through a satellite communication system. The ability of the hardware to store data and process it at a very fast rate helps to deal with the data volumes, its storage and access effectively. The ability of the computer to sort and merge helps to organize the data in a particular manner and process it for complex lengthy computations. Since the computer is capable of digital, graphic, word image, voice and text processing, it is exploited to generate information and present it in the form which is easy to understand for the information user. The ability of a computer system to provide security of data brings a confidence in the management in the storage o data on a magnetic media in an impersonal mode.

The computer system provides the facilities such as READ ONLY where you cannot delete to UPDATE. It provides an access to the selected information through a password and layered access facilities. The confidence nature of the data and information can be maintained in a computer system. With this ability, the MIS become a safe application in the organization. The software, an integral part of a computer system, further enhances the hardware capability. The software is available to handle the procedural and nonprocedural data processing. For example, if you want to use a formula to calculate a certain result, an efficient language is available to handle the situation. If you are not use a formula but have to resort every time to a new procedure, the nonprocedural languages are available. The software is available to transfer the data from one computer system to another. Hence, you can compute the results at one place and transfer them to a computer located at another place for some other use. The computer system being able to configure to the specific needs helps to design a flexible MIS. The advancement in computers and the communication technology has the distance, speed, volume and complex computing an easy task. Hence, designing the MIS for a specific need and simultaneously designing a flexible and open system becomes possible, thereby saving a lot of drudgery of development and maintenance and maintenance of the system. The concept of user . friendly systems and the end user computing is possible, making information processing a personalized function. However, the application of the management principles and practices in today's complex business world is possible only when the MIS is based on computer system support.

MANAGEMENT INFORMATION SYSTEM AND ACADEMICS

The management's information system draws a lot of support from other academic disciplines too. The foundation of MIS is the management theory. It uses the principles and practices of management while designing the system, ant gives due regard to the theory of organizational behavior. It considers the human mind as a processor of information. While designing the report format and forming communication channels, MIS takes into account the behavior of the manager as an individual and in a group. It gives due regard to the personal factors such as bias, thinking with a fixed frame of reference, risk aversion, strengths and weaknesses.

Another area of academics is operational research. The operational research is used for developing the models of management and they are then incorporated in the MIS as decision support systems. The inventory control, queuing theory, and resource programming are used in the MIS as decision support systems. The network theory is used for planning and controlling large projects. The application of PER / CPM to a project planning is now easily possible through the MIS support. In the area of accounting application, it uses the accounting principles to ensure that the data is correct and valid. It uses the principles of double entry bookkeeping for balancing the accounts. It uses the accounting methodology for generating a trial balance sheet and other books of accounts.

The MIS uses the communication theory in a significant manner. The principle of feedback is used while designing analysis. Systems. While designing the report format, attention is paid to avoid noise and distortions in the communication process. The MIS further relies heavily on the decision methodology. It uses different mathematical techniques to handle the situation of decision making uses the method of decision-making under certainty for decision- making and action. The MIS is based on database structures, viz .hierarchical, network and relational database have roots in the mathematics and the set theory.

The MIS becomes rich in content and more useful when it becomes more and more a decision- making or decision- support system. The is possible when it builds decision making systems in MIS which in turn is possible if it draws tools, techniques, methods, rules and principles from pure and application science, and use them as an integral part of the system. The MIS draws data from its own source and uses it in the application of a variety of tools and techniques to solve the management, mathematics, and accounting. Psychology, communication theory, operations research and probability theory for building processes, methods, and decision . support systems in designing business application.

MIS And The User

Every person in the organization is a user of the MIS. The people in the organization operate at all levels in the hierarchy. A typical user is a clerk, an assistant, an officer, an executive or a manager. Each of them has a specific task and a role to play in the management of business. The MIS caters to the needs of all persons. The main task of a clerk is to search the data, make a statement and submit it to the higher level. A clerk can use the MIS for a quick search and reporting the same to higher level. An assistant has the task of collecting and organizing the data, and conducting a rudimentary analysis of integrating the data from different and disciplines to analyze it and make a critical comment if anything adverse is found. The MIS offers the methods and facilities to integrate the data and report the same in a proper format. An executive plays the role of a decision maker. He is in of responsibility and accountability a position of a planner and a decision maker. He is responsible for achieving the target and goals of the organization. The MIS provides facilities to analyze the data and offers the decision support systems to perform the task of execution. The MIS provides an action oriented information.

The manager has a position of responsibility and accountability for the business results. His management role expands beyond his management function. He is a strategist and a long-term planner. He is a person with a foresight, an analytical ability and is expected to use these abilities in the functions of top management. The MIS provides information in a structured or unstructured format for him to react. The MIS caters to his constant changing needs of information. The user of the MIS is expected to be a rational person and the design of the MIS is based on this assumption. However, in reality the impact created on individuals by MIS is difficult to explain. The nature of the impact in a few cases is negative. However, this negative impact can be handled with proper training and counseling. It is observed that at lower level, is a sense of insecurity. As the MIS takes away the drudgery of search, collection, writing and reporting the data, the work vacuum, so created is not easily filled, thus creating a sense of insecurity. To some extent the importance of the person is also lost, giving rise to a fear of non-recognition in the organization.

At the level of an officer and an executive, the MIS does the job the of data manipulation and integration. It analyses the data in a predetermined manner. This means that the knowledge of business is transferred from an individual to the MIS and is made available to all in the organization. This change arising out of the MIS creates a sense of being neglected for knowledge, information and advice. The psychological impact is larger if the person is not able to cope up with this change by expanding or enriching the job and the position held by him. The manager holding a position in the top or middle management suffers from fear of challenge and exposure. The MIS makes these competitors more effective as they have access to the information and have an ability to interpret. This leads to a situation where he is afraid that that his position, decision and defense will be challenged and may be proved wrong sometime. The risk of adverse exposure to the higher management also increases. The effects so far pointed out are all negative and they are seen only in few cases.

The positive effects on the individuals at all levels are that they have become more effective operators. The time and energy which was spent earlier in unproductive work is now applied for a productive work. Some are able to use their analytical skills and knowledge with the in formation support for improving their position in the organization. Managers, having improved their decision . Making ability, are able to handle the complex situations with relative ease. Some are benefited by improving their performance and being held in high esteem by the higher management. The enterprising managers are able to use the systems and the models for trying out a Number of alternatives in a given problem situation. The impact of the MIS on people Of the organization is phenomenal as it has made the same body of people collectively more effective and productive.

The recent major technological advances in communication such as Multimedia, Imaging. Graphical User Interfaces (GUI), Internet, Web etc. and the ability to access the data stored at different locations on the variety hardware of platforms would make MIS more attractive and efficient proposition. An intelligent user of information can demonstrate the ability of decision making, since his manipulative capability is considerably increased, with the information now being available on his desktop. Through the MIS, the information can be used as a strategic weapon to counter the threats to business, make business more competitive, and bring about the organizational transformation through integration. A good MIS also makes an organization seamless by removing all the communication barriers.

2.8 ROLE AND IMPORTANCE OF MANAGEMENT

Management as defined by Mary Follett is the art of getting things done through people. A manger is defined as a person who achieves the organizations goals by motivating others to perform not by performing himself. Whether management is an art or a science is a very subjective question. But it can be said without doubt that modern management in the environment of technology is becoming more of a science than an art. We define management for the purpose of Management information Systems as the process of planning, organizing, staffing, coordinating and controlling the efforts of the members of the organization to achieve common stated goals of the organization.

In the process of management, a manager uses human skills, material resources and scientific methods to perform all the activities leading to the achievement of goals. The management process involves a continuous resolution of conflicts of one kind or the other which affects the achievement of goals. In the management of any activity, a manager comes across human conflict, conflict of goals, between alternative resources, conflict of time, conflict of approach or method and the conflict of choice. The manager uses a variety of tools, techniques and skills while executing the management process of planning, organizing, staffing, coordinating and controlling. An effective way of handling this process is to treat the organization as a system. The result . oriented management approaches the problem of management through the system view of the organization.

The key concepts of the system theory used in the management are as follows:

a. A system is a comprehensive assembly of parts becoming an organization to achieve the stated goals.

b. A system is called OPEN if it has interaction with the environment and CLOSED if it not have an interaction with the environment.

c. A system is defined, described and understood by the boundaries within which it performs.

d. The system are subject to entropy, i..e., the tendency to run down. Closed systems suffer from entropy as they are cut off from the environment, while open systems interact with the environment and draw upon the support of resources to maintain a given condition.

e. Systems try to remain in an equilibrium or a steady state by taking recourse to corrective action.

This is possible when the system has its own feedback, i.e., an informational input about the state of the system. The advantage of viewing the management as a system is that it enables us to see the critical variables, constraints and their interaction with one another. It force the manager to look at the situation in such a way that due regard is given to the consequences arising out of interaction with the related element or subjects. The process of management explained earlier consists of steps which are relationally linked and locked with each other. In the context of the MIS, the systems approach to management is the most efficient one. The understanding of the basic principle of management theory evolved the scholars Henri Fayol, Chester Barnard and Alvin Brown is very much essential. The application of management principles in an environment, recognizing the specific situation, is the accepted practice of management. Deviating from the principle to honour the situation and at the same time not diluting the management principle is the managerial risk.

In the context of the MIS, the systems approach to management is the most efficient one. The understanding of the basic principle of management theory evolved the scholars Henri Fayol, Chester Barnard and Alvin Brown is very much essential. The application of management principles in an environment, recognizing the specific situation, is the accepted practice of management.

Deviating from the principle to honour the situation and at the same time not diluting the management principle is the managerial skill. The manager must have a knowledge of management theory and principle as the skill to use them in a particular environment.

2.9 APPROACHES TO MANAGEMENT

Frederick W Taylor, is recognized as the father of scientific management. His principles can be summarised as follows:

a. Replace the rules of thump with scientific rules.

b. Obtain a harmony in group action.

c. Achieve cooperation of human beings, rather than chaotic individualism.

d. Work for a maximum output .

e. Develop all workers to the possible potential for their own highest possible prosperity.

Table 2.1 *Principles of Operational Management*

Principle	Comments
Division of work	Efficient handling of work.
Authority and responsibility	Pinpoints accountability.
Discipline	Adherence to rules, regulations, norms and priorities.
Unity of command	Single source directed towards one objective.
Unity of direction	Efforts should be directed towards one objective.
Subordination of individual to Corporate interest	Ignore the individual interests for overall betterment of the organization.
Remuneration	Should be fair for maximum satisfaction.
Centralisation	Authority should be centralized just enough for control. Overgeneralization is unproductive.
Scalar chains	Chain of authority vested into the people should not be short-circuited.
Order	Orderly arrangement of men, material and other resources is necessary.
Equity	Subordinates should be dealt with kindliness and justice to elicit loyalty and devotion.
Stability of tenure	It is necessary to ensure that the turnover of people is controlled for stability.
Initiative	The initiative of subordinates should be encouraged, sacrificing personal vanity of the superior.

Fayol regarded the elements of management as planning, organizing, commanding, coordinating and controlling. He believed that the operational management would succeed through the elements of management. During the same period when Taylor, Fayol and others were concentrating on the scientific management, another group of scholars was concentrating on industrial psychology and social theory as the basis for the scientific management.

Robert Owen, Rountree, Lyndall Urwick are credited to evolve the management with a focus on the personal management. Max Weber, Vilfredo Pareto, Mayo Elton are the scholars who thought that productivity can be improved through the social factors as morale and satisfactory relation between the members of work group, and an effective management is possible only if human behavior and group behavior is managed through the interpersonal skills, viz, motivating, counseling, leading and communication. Hawthorne.s studies brought out the theory that man is a .Social Animal. Operating in the socio. Technical system and, therefore, the emphasis in effective management is on behavioral sciences. Chester Barnard advocated the theory od system as an approach to the management. Barnard said that due to the physical and biological limitations of individuals, they cooperate in the work environment. The cooperation increases with effective and efficient incentives. He further said that the cooperation is more effective if the members of the group communicate with one another, are willing to contribute to group.s action, and have a conscious common Purpose. He father said that a groups of peoples in the system work as an organization is looked upon as a system of factions, a system of in a system of incentives, a system of authority and a direction and a system of logical decision making. The emergence of the modern management thought is credited to the social scientists, the behavioral scientists, the systems scientists and the practicing managers.

FUNCTIONS OF THE MANAGER

An individual who gets the thing done is a Manager. It is necessary to distinguish between the task and the functions. While manager may perform the task such as accounting, selling, manufacturing, purchasing, etc. These activities are called as task and not as functions. The activities that are performed through the managerial functions are planning, organization, staffing, directing coordinating and controlling

1. Planning is a process of determining the goals and objectives and evolving strategies policies, programmers and procedures for the achievement of these goals. The essence of the process is decision making as there are a number of alternatives in each of these factors.

2. Organisation involves evolving the structure of the people working in the organization and their roles. It specifies an authority structure and assigns activities to the people backed by the delegation of authority. Building a meaningful effective structure of authority and the relationship is known as organizing.

3. Staffing involves manning the positions in the organization structure. It requires defining the manpower needs per position or centre of activity. It requires appropriate selection of the person or persons ensuring that they together will achieve the goals and objectives of the organization.

4. Directing is a complex task of implementing the process of management. In the process, the manger is required to guide, clarify and solve the problems of the people and their activities. It

is necessary to motivate the people to work for the goal with an interest and a confidence.

5. Coordinating is the function which brings a harmony and smoothness in the various group activities and individual efforts directed towards the accomplishment of goals. It is a process of synchronizing individual actions and the efforts which may differ because of the differences in the personal goals and the common goals, the differences in the interpretation of methods and directions. It is, therefore, necessary to undertake centrally a process of coordinating and reconciling the differences in the approach, timing, efforts and interests towards a common goal. This task is to be carried out by the authority placed at a higher level in the organization structure

6. Controlling is a process of measurement of an output, comparing it with the goals, the objectives and the target, and taking corrective actions, if the output is falling short of the stated norms. Controlling ensures an achievement of the plan. The essence of the control lies in good planning. It helps to evaluate the performance, highlights abnormal deviations, and guides a manager to take specific corrective actions. This may call for a change of plan, a reallocation of resources, a modification of methods, procedures and even the organization structure. The control is central to the managerial function. The manager.s main function, therefore, is planning and control of the business

functions and operations. While performing these functions, he resorts to the scientific approach to the management.

2.10 Managers And The Environment

All managers, whether they are managing a business, a school, a hospital, Government Department, or any enterprise, work in an environment in which the organization operates. There are a number of forces which are generated in the environment, which have an impact on the managerial performance. These forces may be from within or from outside the organization. They affect, directly or indirectly, the process of the management and a manager is required to meet these forces effectively. While to some extent the internal environment is controllable, the external environment is beyond his control. Since it is proven that the external environment also has an impact on the business manager.s performance, it is necessary to know and understand the environment. For the purpose of discussion, the external environment is classified into five classes as the economic, the technological, the social, the political and the ethical environment.

Economic Environment

The economic environment comprises capital, labor, price changes, productivity, fiscal and monetary policy and customers.

Capital

It is required to run the organization. The enterprise needs a long-term and a shortterm capital. The capital required can be either from the internal sources or borrowed from the financial institutions. When a capital is borrowed, it is borrowed at an interest. The organization is forced to borrow for various reasons and the interest charged by the lending financial institutions forms the cost of the capital. Hence management of the capital is an important aspect of the business.

LABOR

The next important cost of a business is the cost of labor. The cost of labor is determined every two three years by a union agreement. The settlement of an agreement is based on the cost of living index, the industry wage standards, the availability of labor, etc. These aspects are external to the organization and a manager has no control on them.

PRICE CHANGES

Price changes occur in the economy for various reasons. The changes occur because of decrease in the demand and supply, the changes in the consumer behavior, in the consumption pattern and the money supply, and so on. The price changes affect the cost of raw material and labor and on these changes a manager has no control.

PRODUCTIVITY

Productivity is a result of the capital, labor and technology. Many a times and organizations business are taken over by better technology. The costs are affected by the technology changes affecting the productivity. The manager has to respond quickly to the technological changes to save the business.

FISCAL AND MONETARY POLICY

The Government announces fiscal policies and controls them. The organizations profit position is affected by these policies. These policies affect the credit terms, the price of the inputs and the money supply affecting the cash position of the organization. A manager has a very little leverage to deal with these policy changes.

CUSTOMERS

The customers rule the business, especially when the business operates in a buyers market. In a competitive world, it is very difficult to predict the customer behavior. The changes in the demands occur with growth and technology. The customer does not show consistent preference to the product. The change in the business orientation to suit the changes in the consumer demand is a difficult task for the manager. It is not always possible to predict these changes well in advance in order to take any managerial action to meet the changed situation.

TECHNOLOGICAL ENVIRONMENT

The technology has a major impact on the business. It affects the business prospects, cuts down the profits and forces the management to change the course of the business operations. It requires changes in the product design and promotes new concepts. It generates new business opportunities. Any change in technology changes the work culture, the methods and the systems. It affects the speed of the operations and gives a boost to the productivity of the production systems. Examples of technological changes are seen in aviation, electronics, energy, communication, consumer goods industry, optics, medicines and manufacturing.

SOCIAL ENVIRONMENT

The social environment is built around the attitudes, the desires, the expectations, the degree of intelligence and education, the beliefs and customs, the religion, the caste and creed of the people. The social environments are built in centuries and hence it is deeply rooted in the society. The social environment has an important impact on the business and the organizational productivity. Social factors create an attitude towards the work, generate the product choices, and manipulate the consumer behavior. It is well known that it took a lot of time to convince the farmers in India about the use of fertilizers. It is recognized that rural marketing is different from the urban marketing. In spite of the technological advances, frozen foods are not finding consumer preferences. Introduction of computers in the service industry is still a difficult proposition. A number of such examples can be cited to prove that the social environment affects business and makes the managers task very difficult and challenging.

POLITICAL ENVIRONMENT

The political factor is the most important factor which affects the business in Indian environment. The unstable political environment brings stagnancy in the business development. The changes in ruling party bring economic policy changes, affecting the business. The sect oral preferences, such as an agricultural versus an industrial, an educational versus a basic research, an investment in the service sector versus a core sector come about with change in the ruling political party and its policies. Such changes have a long-term impact on business performance. The manager has to deal with such changes effectively.

ETHICAL ENVIRONMENT (SYSTEMS OF A MORAL BEHAVIOR)

Some business problems arise due to failing on the ethical grounds. The government has enacted many laws and regulations to bring about harmonious operations in business. However, some aspects of the business operations are left as ethics, called the business ethics. The business ethics emerge from the professional conduct, the business norms and codes on confidentiality, the payment and documentation, the adherence to generally accepted standards of accounting and auditing. Business ethics is a set of norms which are universally accepted as a business behavior. All these factors discussed so far, are beyond the control of the manager. At best he can predict, assess, evaluate and take such actions which will help him to control the situation.

2.11 MANAGEMENT AS A CONTROL SYSTEM

Planning, organizing, staffing, coordinating, directing and controlling are the various Steps in a management process. All the steps prior to a control are necessary but are not necessarily self-assuring the results unless it is followed by a strong control mechanism. The management experts have viewed these steps as Management Control System. They postulate the hypothesis that unless a control is exercised on the process, the goals will not be achieved. They advocate a system of effective control to ensure the achievement of the business objectives.

A definition of control is the process through which managers assure that actual activities conform to the planned activities, leading to the achievement of the stated common goals. The control process measures a progress towards those goals, and enables the manager to detect the deviations from the original plan in time to take corrective actions before it is too late.

Robert J Mockler defines and points out the essential elements of the control process.

The management is a systematic effort to set the performance standards in line with the performance objectives, to design the information feedback systems, to compare the actual performance with these predetermined standards, to identify the deviations from the standards, to measure its significance and to take corrective actions in case of significant deviations. This systematic effort is undertaken through the management control system.

The control system is essential to meet the environmental changes discussed earlier, to meet the complexity of today.s business, to correct the mistakes made by the people, and to effectively monitor the delegation process. A reliable and effective control system has the following features.

EARLY WARNING MECHANISM

This is a mechanism of predicting the possibility of achieving the goals and the standards before it is too late and allowing the manager to take corrective actions.

PERFORMANCE STANDARD

The performance standard must be measurable and acceptable to all the organization. The system should have meaningful standards relating to the work areas, responsibility, and managerial functions and so on. Fro example, the management would have standards relating to the business performance, such as production, sales, inventory, quality, etc. The operational management would have standards relating to the shift production, rejections, down time, utilization of resources, sale in a typical market segment and so. On. The chain of standards, when achieved, will ensure an achievement of the goals of the organization.

STRATEGIC CONTROLS

In every business there are strategic areas of control knows as the critical success factors. The system should recognize them and have controls instituted on them.

FEEDBACK

The control system would be effective; it continuously monitors the performance and sends the information to the control centre for action. It should not only highlight the progress but also the deviations.

ACCURATE AND TIMELY

The feedback should be accurate in terms of results and should be communicated on time for corrective action.

REALISTIC

The system should be realistic so that the cost of control is far less than the benefits. The standers are realistic and are believed as achievable. Sufficient incentive and rewards are to be provided to motivate the people.

The Information Flow

The system should have the information flow aligned with the organization structure and the decision makers should ensure that the right people get the right information for action and decision making.

Exception Principle

The system should selectively approve some significant deviations from the performance standards on the principle of management by exception. A standard is control system has a set of objectives, standards to measure, a feedback mechanism and an action centre as elements of the system. They need to be properly evolved and instituted in the organization with due recognition to the internal and the external environment. The system as a whole should be flexible to be change with ease so that the impact of changed environment is handled effectively.

Management By Exception

Pareto.s principle of 80:20 applications to the management of enterprise. Several terms have been coined on this principle such as management by objectives; management methodology is the **management by exception**. When the management operates under time constraint, each manager has to him to attend to the situation where his attention is necessary. Such attention would lead to an action, a decision or a wait . and- see approach.

If all the situations are considered in a routine manner, it consumes time and tends to be neglected over a period of time. An efficient manager tries for selective attention to manage within the available time resource. The principle evolved, therefore, is of the management by exception. The exception is decided the impact a situation would make on the performance, the process and the standards set in the management control system. The exception is defined as a significant deviation from the performance, or the process and the standard. The deviation could be abnormal on a positive or on a negative side of the standard. The deviation could be predictive or could be arising out of random causes in the business operations. IT is, therefore, necessary to assess whether the deviation is sporadic or consistently coming in, calling for managerial attention. The manager is interested in knowing the significant deviation by the yardsticks of consistency and not out of random causes. The significant deviations are exceptional in nature and require to be attended to immediately. A manager is further interested in knowing the reasons behind the exceptional nature of the situation. It is possible to trace the reasons of deviation, and it is possible to take a corrective action. The significant deviation can occur on account of wrong performance standards and wrong management process. Many times standards are set very low and they need to be looked in to avoid the misuse of resources. If the standards are set too high, then the people fail to achieve them on account of de motivating factor of the high standards. A wrong management process refers to a variety of decisions a manager has taken in the planning, organization, staffing, directing and controlling a given management task. These decisions relate to the choice and the allocation of resources, the methods of using resources, the application of the tools and the techniques, the use of manpower by way of staffing and the manner in which the efforts are coordinated in the organization. For an efficient and an effective management, without loss of time, it is, therefore, necessary to report the significant deviations to the right person in the organization. In this regard a manager himself has to provide the conditions of exceptions in the control system so that they are highlighted and informed. The management by exception commands grip on the management process. The managerial effort gets directed towards the goal with the purpose of achievement.

2.12 MIS: A SUPPORT TO THE MANAGEMENT

The management process is executed through a variety of decisions taken at each step of planning organizing, staffing, directing, coordinating and control. As discussed in Chapter 1, the MIS aids decision making. If the management is able to spell out the decisions required to taken in these steps are tabulated in **Table 2.2.**

Table 2.2 Decisions in Management

Steps in management	Decision
Planning	A selection from various alternatives- strategies, resources, methods, etc.
Organization	A selection of a combination out of several combinations of the goals, people, resources, method, and authority.
Staffing	Providing a proper manpower complement.
Directing	Choosing a method from the various methods of directing the efforts in the organization.
Coordinating	Choice of the tools and the techniques for coordinating the efforts for optimum results.
Controlling	A selection of the exceptional conditions and the decision guidelines.

Table 2.2 Decisions in Management

Steps in management Decision

➤ Planning A selection from various alternatives- strategies, resources, methods, etc.

➤ Organization A selection of a combination out of several combinations of the goals, people, resources, method, and authority. Staffing Providing a proper manpower complement.

➤ Directing Choosing a method from the various methods of directing the efforts in the organization.

➤ Coordinating Choice of the tools and the techniques for coordinating the efforts for optimum results.

➤ Controlling A selection of the exceptional conditions and the decision guidelines.

The objective of the MIS is to provide information for a decision support in the process of management. It should help in such a way that the business goals are achieved in the most efficient manner. Since the decision making is not restricted to a particular level, the MIS is expected to support all the levels of the management in conducting the business operations. Unless the MIS becomes a management aid, it is not useful to the organization.

2.13 MANAGEMENT AND MANAGEMENT INFORMATION SYSTEMS

- Environment
- Management
- Goal Setting

MIS: A SUPPORT TO THE MANAGEMENT

The management process is executed through a variety of decisions taken at each step of planning organizing, staffing, directing, coordinating and control. As discussed in Chapter 1, the MIS aids decision making. Decisions in Management Steps in management Decision Planning A selection from various alternatives- strategies, resources, methods, etc.

Organization A selection of a combination out of several combinations of the goals, people, resources, method, and authority. Staffing Providing a proper manpower complement. Directing Choosing a method from the various methods of directing the efforts in the organization. Coordinating Choice of the tools and the techniques for coordinating the efforts for optimum results. Controlling A selection of the exceptional conditions and the decision guidelines.

The objective of the MIS is to provide information for a decision support in the process of management. It should help in such a way that the business goals are achieved in the most efficient manner. Since the decision making is not restricted to a particular level, the MIS is expected to support all the levels of the management in conducting the business operations. Unless the MIS becomes a management aid, it is not useful to the organization.

Business plan	MIS plan
Business goals and objectives.	Management information system, objectives, consistent to the business goals and objectives.
Business plan and strategy.	Information strategy for the business plan implementation playing a supportive role.
Strategy planning and decisions.	Architecture of the Management Information System to support decisions.
Management plan for execution and control.	System development schedule, matching the plan execution.
Operation plan for the execution.	Hardware and software plan for the procurement and the implementation.

PROCESS OF MANAGEMENT EFFECTIVESS

Negandhi Estafen. provides a good model for the analysis of management effectiveness which generates enterprise effectiveness in achieving the goals and objectives. The model puts a lot of emphasis on the management philosophy and the environment factors on which the effectiveness is dependent. The environment factors provide the opportunities to survive and grow with certain constraints, while the management philosophy sets the guidelines for deciding the management practices to run the enterprise. While the environment factors are difficult to control, it is left for the management to change its philosophy towards the various players in the business, viz. the employees, the consumers the suppliers, the government, the community and the shareholders. Basically, It is a change in attitude towards these players. For example, how to look at the employees?

If the attitude is to treat them as business partners, you will empower them and create a sense of belonging to the organization. Such an attitude will have impact on the management practices, where the employee will play a decisive critical role. It will affect the organization structure by reducing its size and the reporting levels. If the attitude towards the consumer is changed to fulfill the expectations giving rise to a higher satisfaction, then the management practices in the product design, manufacturing and marketing will undergo a significant change. The product life cycle will then be short, and more features and functions will be added to the product fulfilling not only the functional needs but also the service needs of the consumer.

The management practices therefore emerge out of the managements philosophy and the environment, in which it operates. The management effectiveness would largely depend on both these factors. The MIS design would therefore, be different depending upon the management practices followed by several organization in the same industry. Such design improves the management effectiveness leading to an improvement in the enterprise effectiveness.

2.14 GOALS, OBJECTIVES AND TARGETS

The process of management begins with setting of goals, objectives and targets The goals are long- term aims to be achieved by the organization objective are relatively short . term milestones to be accomplished, while the targets generally refer to physical achievements in the organizations business. The goals, objectives and targets are so set they are consistent with each other and help to achieve each other and help to achieve each other. The are to be achieved within a stipulated time and failing to achieve the same, means loss of business profit and image. The difference between these entities can be best understood by examples in the three types of organizations given in Table The setting of goals, objectives and targets is a top management function. It has its implications on the business operations and profits. These are set considering the environment and changes expected to occur in about five to six years. The organization is expected to consider and cater for these changes and translate them into business operations. The setting of goals objective and targets helps to pull the resources of the organization in one direction and solve. It help to build the strategies, frame the polices and set the rules of conducting the business. It provides an efficient measure to monitor the managerial process. The people in the organization can have common understanding of the purpose of the business operations. In an organization as time progresses, business goals, departmental goals, functional goals and personal goals emerge, which create conflicting environment in the organization. The goals, objective and targets from a network. Achievement of targets helps in accomplishing objective and accomplishment of objectives leads to the attainment of goals. Careful determination of these entities is therefore essential for a successful management process. The goals objectives and targets become reference points for strategic planning and operations planning. If further helps the management to identify key areas of business and key areas of management attention. It helps appropriates and consistent business review. The performance appraisal of the manager becomes impersonal and unbiased as it is done with reference to achievement of goals, objective and targets. McGreor saw appraisal against the goals and objective are necessary in every area where performance and results directly and vitally affect the survival growth and prosperity of business.

PLANNING

Planning is basic to all managerial functions. It is a process of selecting one course of action from different alternatives, for achieving the stated goals, objective and targets. It is a decision making process determining in advance what to do, when to do, how to do what is to do. Planning creates a frame of activity and events which are to happen or a runway for achieving corporate goals, objective and targets. Planning process demands resource allocation through decision making. The organization may have a plan; but question is how effective the plan is. The efficiency of a plan is measured by the amount it contributes towards achievement of goals. The plan is efficient the goals with less investment or with less resources. Therefore, efficient planning involves selecting a plan among several alternative plans. An efficient plan enables the management to handle uncertainty and risk in the business.

It helps to handle the change occurring in the environment and affecting the plan itself. Planning helps to make operations economical as it continuously evaluates the costs and outputs and forces optimum use resources. It further helps to control business operations at all levels with Common reference to goals, objectives and targets. Planning is a process and hence it has a methodology. The first step in planning forecasting the environment, in which the plan is to be made and operated. Forecasting provides information on population, growth price trends, market changes, and new opportunities, changes in technology the plan will be developed and implemented. The second step in planning is determining alternative courses of action. The management.s ability lies in creating a number of alternatives. The effective way of creating a number of alternatives is to build models of the situation and use it as a tool for the generation of alternatives. These models. Are known as system models, operational research model and mathematical models. Consequent o the development of alternative courses of actions, the necessity is to analyze the feasibility of each. As, a modek can give infinite alternatives, only some of them can be feasible in the given conditions and constraints. The constraints may be man-made or environmental; but they affect the feasibility of the action. Evaluating the feasibility of each alternative brings the infinite number of alternatives to a limited number. The third step in the planning process is to evaluate the best among all the feasible alternatives. The analysis and evaluation is done with reference to the objectives such as, minimization of cost, maximization of profit, yield, and productivity, etc. The right choice of an objective is a crucial factor in the selection process. The planning begins with the setting of goals and objectives and ends up in selecting the most rational course of action.

As mentioned earlier, the organization has a network of goals, objectives and targets. It is necessary to develop the network of plans corresponding to this network. The process leads to the development of corporate plans, investment plans, marketing plans, and advertising plans. Normally, the corporate plans are for a longer period and the derived plans are for shorter periods. Since the plan has a commitment to time, it is necessary to build a flexible plan capable of undergoing a suitable change to alter the goals and objectives within the same time. The flexibility, as possible, should be built in, so that the cost of changes is not very high and the implementation is still possible without loss of time. The implementation of plans is made through developing the strategies, policies, systems, rules, procedures, programmers and the budgets. The strategy shows the direction, focus, emphasis and development of resources. Many a times good plans fail because of strategic failure. The purpose of the strategy is not to outline a precise method of implementation but to provide a boost or thrust to the plans of implementation. An appropriate strategy helps to cut down the use of resources and accelerates the process of achieving the goals.

The policy is a statement of management which stands on the top of all plans or courses of action. A rational plan or a decision can be rejected on the premise of policy .The policies are evolved in the wider frame of strategies and are generally not questionable; but these can be changed. For example, the organization can have a policy of recruiting personnel only with the qualification of MBA or it may have a policy of changing the prices once a year and not too frequently. The policy, therefore, is a general guideline and is to be followed by all.

The system is a vehicle for the implementation of a plan. The system provides pathways, gates and structures for communication and control. The strategies and policies are important for successful implementation of the plans. Depending upon the plans, systems will be built as closed or open systems. The rules, procedures and programmers help to implement the operational plans. They provide a common basis and an understanding of conducting business operations. A strict adherence to the rules and the procedures builds discipline in the organization. A smooth implementation of the plan calls for the rules, procedures and programmers to be observed properly. When the organization becomes bigger, the adherence to rules procedures and systems brings a higher degree of formalization in the process of implementation.

The effectiveness of the plan depends on how it is implemented. A successful implementation requires appropriate timing of launching the basic plan and its derivatives. Lack of knowledge creates the problems of going away in a totally different direction. The plan must be evolved by people who are going to implement it. Their participation brings their involvement and commitment to the plan. For effective planning, participation should be encouraged. An effective planning should begin at the top and flow down the line. The effectiveness is brought in by taking a series of decisions, committing resources, giving directions, and executing controls to achieve the goals and objectives. The process planning, therefore, is to develop the alternatives based on some choice about goals. It the situation is that of uncertainty, then the evaluation is done through risk analysis ad preference theory using utility as criteria.

ORGANISING

Organizing is an important step in the managerial process and relates to the people in an enterprise. It deals with a quantitative and a qualitative aspect of manpower in terms of placement, the roles they and the relations amongst them, with the aim that they work together effectively towards accomplishing the goals, objectives and the targets of the organization. In essence, it deals with organizing the manpower resources for a given plan of execution.

The organization could be formal or informal. The organization is formal when the roles, the relations of the people and the objectives they should achieve well defined. In an informal organization, it is left to the people to understand and evolve suitable roles and relationships to achieve the objectives.

While creating the organization is given to an appropriate splitting of the enterprise activities, by way of function, and grouping them in such a way that they form a division, a department, a section or a formal group. The people heading these entities should have enough authority to decide, and should exercise a discretion in using the authority. The people should and the members of the structure of roles and relationships that it is designed to work effectively and the members of the structure are able to contribute substantially towards the achievement of goals. The structure would be productive, if it is manned properly. The process of manning involves selecting people in right number and placing them at appropriate levels.

Peter Drucker recommends three ways to determine the structure:

- Activity analysis
- Decision analysis, and
- Relations analysis

Organizing is a process by which the manager can bring a smoothness of operations, by way of conflict resolution, assigning work responsibility, and creating appropriate work environment of teamwork while deciding on the process of organizing. There are certain important factors to which attention should be paid and which are discussed as follows.

ORGANISATION LEVELS AND THE SPAN OF CONTROL

This factor deals with grouping the people in hierarchical form, determining the levels in the organization. The levels get determined by the spa of control, i.e., in the organization how many subordinates a superior can mange. This number can vary anywhere between four to eight in higher levels of management and eight to fifteen in lower levels of management to be taken, and the strengths and weaknesses of the people and the degree of the delegation of the responsibilities that a superior is willing to attain. The span of control can be increased and the number the levels can be brought down by training the subordinates, precise planning, use of objective standards, effective communications and formalizing the administration by way of rules, programmers and policies.

DEPARTMENTATION

Departmentaton is a process of breaking an enterprise into smaller groups and levels. There is a number of ways to break the enterprise. A widely accepted is by functions of the enterprise, viz., Marking, Production, Finance, Personnel, Materials, etc. The second method is based on geographic area distribution. This method is resorted to when the distances are long, the activities are many and the decision making is decentralized. Many organizations have divisions, branches and territories through which the business operations are conducted.

The third method to department is by way of the product or the services the organization is providing. The department of the organization brings operational convenience, creates appropriate responsibility centers, facilitates a formal and an informal communication, permits an evaluation of activities by a smaller group, and provides control and decision points for the top management. Each method of a departmentalizing has advantages and disadvantages and, therefore, it is to be chosen based on the needs of the management.

RELATIONS OF LINE AND STAFF FUNCTIONS

The function of a department can be as a line or a staff. The functions which have a direct responsibility of achieving the targets for production or sales are line functions. The staff functions are those which do not participate directly in the activity but aid line functions to achieve the targets. Production Planning, Marketing, Purchasing, etc, are staff functions. The distinction is more clear and precise at higher levels. The staff function is advisory but owns the responsibility for the results and is accountable for on performance. The relationship between the line and the staff functions is always strained. The performance of the line function depends upon how the staff function has planned the activities. Deficient planning leads to an initialization of line capacity and non attainment of targets. A line function does not have resources, leverages and powers to overcome the problems arising out of the staff functions.

The function either is a line function a staff function; but still it requires decision making. As one person cannot plan, execute and control all the tasks in the functions, owing to the   imitations of time and capacity, it is necessary that the decision making is not centralized at one point. Handing over limited authority of decision making to the subordinated is called delegation. The concept of delegation is based on the premise that an individual can take decision if supported by information, knowledge and guidance, and is motivated enough to perform. The concept of delegation accepts the responsibility of non-performance of the delegated person or the mistakes made by him. Hence, most routine types of decisions are delegated with the support of rules, conditions and the method of decision making.

The failures in delegation occur not because of the lack of understanding of the principle of delegation, but because of the inability to implement it into practice. A lot depends upon the ability of the manager to delegate and upon the capabilities of the subordinates to use the authority. The manager is not able to delegate, if he does not have a positive attitude towards delegation, if e is not receptive to the subordinates. ideas and is not welling to accept the risk of failure or mistake of his subordinates. A failure to use the delegated authority emanates from a lack communication, guidance, training and motivation.

Towards Effective Organisation

Organisation is an activity of building a structure of roles and relations of the people to secure coordination of individual efforts to achieve common stated goals, objectives and targets. The failure in organization occurs due to the failure to plan properly, to delegate the authority and due to the confusion of relation and authority. The failure also occurs on account of imbalance in the line and staff function and their relation. Organisation becomes effective, if it is designed for the unity of goals and objectives with precise planning and optimum span of control. It becomes further effective, if it works on the principle of command, delegation and parity of authority and responsibility. It becomes productive if it flexible enough to change and is headed by a manager with leadership qualities.

Staffing

The function of staffing deals with manning the enterprise as per the organization structure so that they together implement the process of the management. Staffing involves not only selection of a person but also appraisal and development so that they perform their designated roles. The selection of a person is a difficult task. However, the chances of selecting a wrong person are very less if a proper method is used. Since people cannot be easily replaced because of socio-political and legal reasons, their selection, in terms of quality and, is of paramount importance.

Staffing of enterprise should be for todays as well as that of the future. The requirement of the future is difficult to predict in precise and this requirement needs to be forecasted for more than five to six years. So the purpose of staffing is not manning for the current plan of business but to create a manpower potential capable of undergoing development, so that the same manpower is able to perform the changed roles in the future. Hence the selection of a person in terms of age, qualification and potential becomes an important task in human resource development. The selection of individuals for line functions is not that difficult because the role and the asks are well defined and do not undergo any significant change over a period of time.

- The difficult lies in the selection of management positions. The manager is a multifaceted personality. A person is said to have good managerial potential, if he has the following qualities apart from the function knowledge.

- The person must have the desire to manage.

- He must have the necessary drive and self- motivation to manage.

- He must be able t identify himself with the corporate goals and be committed to them.

- The person must have the capability of applying knowledge to real life situations in the right perspective, locating the problem areas and generating a number of alternate courses of action. In short, he must be a person with analytical ability.

- The person must be able to perform effectively. This is possible only if he has the ability to communicate effectively. If not properly communicated, his ideas and management plans cannot take off. For good communication skills, the person must have a good command but due to the psychological barriers he cannot communicate. These barriers come on account of personality conflicts, power game and dissatisfaction on rewards and promotion.

- The manager must be a person of integrity.
- He should be honest, trustworthy and high achiever. This can be judged by the track record of the person and his work experience and the extra curricular activities he may be performing. The staffing, therefore, deals with creation of human resource in the enterprise to achieve goals, objectives and targets set by the top management.

COORDINATING AND DIRECTING

After organizing the resources and staffing the planned activities, the business plan is launched. The process of implementing the plan is dynamic. It calls upon the manager to perform a number of things in a coordinated manner so that the plan remains valid and the development takes place as per the plan. The process meets with a number of difficulties and the manager is supposed to resolve them. There will be a lag and lead in many activities. There could be shortfalls and overruns. There could be sudden developments which may disturb the plans and the process of implementation. The managers role, in this situation, is to coordinate all the activities and provide leadership to the group to keep the plan moving. Directing and leading are the methods, whereby the subordinates are lead to understand the purpose of the activity, and by way of guidance, a direction is given to them to march towards the goals. Their difficult and conflicts are resolved, bottlenecks removed and a clear path is created to progress on plan achievement. The task of directing and leading becomes more effective if the human side of the enterprise is taken care of by motivating the people. The manager is required to create an environment in which everybody can perform their best. The work environment becomes conducive to good performance if work becomes satisfying and provides an opportunity to expand the scope of work and his influence.

The manager is a leader if he possesses the art of influencing the subordinates in such a way that they willingly perform towards the achievement of the goals, objectives and targets. The process of coordinating and directing takes place through communication. Good communication has been defined by the American Society of Training Directives as an interchange of thought or information to bring about mutual understanding and confidence or good human relations. The coordinating and directing effect is more effective if the manger is able to motivate the subordinates and provide leadership by way of an affective communication.

CONTROLLING

The last but the most important step in the process of management is controlling, the successful execution of management plan. Without control, the process becomes unproductive. The purpose of control is to regulate the process in such a way that the management process continuously strives for the achievement of the goals, objectives and targets.

The control is exercised through a system. The system measures the performance of the management in terms of some predefined measures of output. It compares the output with the standard, identifies the deviations from the standard, and corrects the management process to ensure that the plan continues to be effective in terms of achieving goals, objectives and targets.

The control system work on the principle of feedback. The feedback on the performance should be quick without any loss of time, that corrective action can be taken immediately. The process of correction involves change in the plan, reallocation of resources, application of new system, procedures and rules. The best control is the one which brings the process back into operation on the main track without outside intervention. The control system must get into action automatically to correct the midstream adverse development. Time is the essence of control. If the corrective action is taken late on account of delayed feedback, it is ineffective and may result in heavy losses. Most of the managers look for real time control system, a system which provides an instant negative feedback from the standard and an instantaneous corrective action without any time delay. Since the management control systems are not physical system, where one can desire real time control mechanism, the managers look for feed forward control. The feed forward control gives an advance warning, an indication that the deviations are likely to occur in near future calling for a corrective action. The techniques used in the feed forward control are forecasting, trend analysis and judging the performance from the standpoint of input versus output.

Auditing is also a tool of control. There are several types of audits possible in a business organization. Managerial audit deals with how effectively the plans are made and implemented. It is addressed to the managerial performance to judge whether it was up to the mark, and whether there are any lapses, failures or weaknesses. The operational audit deals with an adherence to the rules and the policies of the management. It identifies whether the operations of the organization are being carried out as per the managerial directives, rules and policies. The financial audit addresses the business and financial transactions to find out whether they are carried out with due regard to the accounting principle and statutes. It also examines whether all the transactions are covered completely and for the year. With the advancement of information technology and computers, a variety of planning and control tools have been developed. Planning and budget models, financial models, risk analysis models, PERT/ CPM, operations research models are some of the examples of the control tools.

2.15 MIS: A TOOL FOR MANAGEMENT PROCESS

The process of management requires a lot of data and information for execution of the plan. This requirement arises on account of that in each step of management, a variety of decisions are taken to correct the course of development. The decisions or actions are prompted due to the feedback given by the control system incorporated in the management system. The control of overall performance is made possible by way of budget summaries and reports. The summary showing sales, costs, profit and return on investment throws light on the direction the organization is moving to. The exception reports identify the weaknesses in the system of management. If effective management system is to be assured, it has to rest on business information. The management performance improves if the business risk and uncertainties are handled effectively. If the information provided is adequate, one can deal with these factors squarely. The information support improves the lack of knowledge, enriches experience and improves analytical abilities leading to better business judgment. So, if efficient information support is to be provided, it calls for a system with the goals of generating management information. A good MIS must furnish information to the managers to expand their knowledge base. He must know the adverse trends in business, the shortfalls and failures in the management process.

Fig. 4.7

The MIS should provide the support to act and decisively. It should support management in terms of basic business information at the corporate level and meet the specific needs of the managers. It should highlight on the critical success factors and support key areas of management. MIS should have, wherever possible, support systems to help the manager in decision making. Modern management systems rely on MIS. The complexity of business operations with skill and foresight to avert the crisis. Modern business management requires shift from the traditional controls to managerial control. The shift requires the manager to become more efficient in handling the he is entrusted with. The manager becomes more efficient if he is well informed, made richer in knowledge, experience and analytical skills and is able to face the uncertainties and the risk of business. This is possible only if he is supported by MIS in his specific task of management of business. Modern business has business has become more technology- oriented wherein the manager is required to be up- to- date on technological advancement not only in his field of operations but also in the other technologies . The emerging new technologies are posing threats to current business and are opening new opportunities for new business ventures. The manager has to keep himself abreast on the information of how these technologies affect his business prospects. A good MIS designed for such a support is absolutely essential. MIS therefore, is a tool for effective execution of the management process.

Unit III

3.1 BASIC MODEL OF ORGANISATION STRUCTURE

The word organization means two things. The first meaning of the word organization is an institution or a functional group. A business organization a hospital, a school a university is some such institution keeping in view the concept of division of labor, authority, responsibility and decision making so that the institution as a stable system, works coherently towards the achievement of goals. .the level at which a person is holding position. The authority is measured on the basis of command on control of resources, the risk of business, and the decision making power to manage the risk and reward. When the authority. Is distributed in a vertical order in terms of levels, the organization is built on the principle of hierarchy of authority. The effectiveness of the authority is based on the span of control, i.e., the number of person being managed and controlled by a person. Depending on the organization, and business, the span may differ from four to seven. The span outside this range has proved to be unproductive and inefficient.

The organization structure is built by arrangement of organizational subsystems. The organization structure is built on four basic principles, viz. hierarchy of authority, specialization, standardization or formalization and, centralization. The structure is built to achieve goals and objectives fitting into the environment. The structure built on any principle shows division of work, managerial and non- managerial manpower allocation as well as flows of decision responsibility and exchange of information. Hierarchy of Authority The authority rests with the individual in the organization. The degree and strength of authority depends on the level at which a person is holding position. The authority is measured on the basis of command on control of resources, the risk of business, and the decision making power to manage the risk and rewards. When the authority is distributed in a vertical order in terms of levels, the organization is built on the principle of hierarchy of authority. The effectiveness of the authority is based on the span of control, i.e., the number of persons being managed and controlled by a person. Depending on the organization, and business, the span may differ from four to seven. The span outside this range has proved to be unproductive and inefficient.

SPECIALIZATION

The second principal of building organization structure is specialization. Specialization can be decided in a number of ways, arranging all similar and associated tasks under one head. For example, a business organization can be structured on the specialization such as Manufacturing, Marketing, Accounting and Personal. A hospital can be structured on the basis of specialization such as General Medicine, Surgery, function, helps to select right people and group them properly, aids in functional planning and control of the activities of the organization.

Standardization (Formalization)

The purpose of standardization or formalization is to make a person in an organization independent, whereby the interaction between the individuals in the organization is minimum. The people work on the basis of rules. Procedures, systems, guidelines and policies. If the degree of such specialization is very high a person can supervise more number of people. In other words, it affects the of control. Favorably. With specialization, the delegation of work and its control has become easier. Where standardization is not possible owing to the nature of business, the risk in business and decision making complexity span of control is reduced as the number of people handle similar range of operations. Requirement of manpower then increases making the organization top heavy.

Centralization

Centralization refers to the location or position where the decision-making centre is localized. In a highly centralized organization, the decision making is at the top and in a decentralized organization; it is delegated down the lien in the organization hierarchy. When business risks are high and difficult to manage, the organization emerges as centralized. The organization is structured on the basis of the above four principles. The blend of these principal is decided on the nature of business, risk of business, size of business, management style and the environment of business. The blending of these principles would undergo a charge as the business grows. The organization is under a continuous process of change to meet the changing needs of business, the organization will have a different structure in its various business stages namely, inception, growth, maturity, and decline. The structure of organization affects organizational productivity, individual performance, growth of human resource, and the manpower itself. A considerable amount of saving in manpower and overhead expenses is possible, if the organization is property structured to the business needs and towards fulfilling the objectives.

Independent of the blend of these principles, the effectiveness of the structure largely depends on the quality of people . ability, skills, knowledge attitude and motivation. The basic model of the organization structure is shown in Fig. 4.1 it shows the arrangement of the people in a reverse tree structure. The basic model will have more levels if the size of the organization is very large. The number of levels will be determined on the basis of the span of control and the nature of work. The appropriateness of the structure can be decided based on the factors like responsibility and authority, economy in conducting the business, the ability to achieve the goals and objectives, a smooth flow of information exchange and communication.

There are four variations of the basic model which are widely used in real life.

3.2 MODIFICATIONS TO THE BASIC MODEL OF ORGANISATION STRUCTURE

There are four modifications to the basic model of organization as under.

1. Functional

2.Product / Market / Service

3. Project

4. Matrix.

FUNCTIONAL ORGANISATION

The functional organization is most suitable where the organization business can be split into clear divisions of activity and all of them are equally important. For example, the business organization can be functionally organized into four or five functions such as marketing manufacturing, finance, personnel, and materials.

Functional organization (Emphasis on functional Management) The strength of the people and the hierarchy in each of the functional organizations would vary depending upon the size and the number of activities. Decision making in any functional organization is at the level of the functional head with accountability to the chief of the organization. The implications of the decisions are largely on the functions themselves. A decision affecting other functions of the business, however, is referred to the top management. The information flow is from the top to the bottom and in the reverse order. The information flow across the functions is not expected. Accumulation of information is at the chief executives level and is shared by the others. The functional organization is most suited where each function is a specialty and calls for an expertise in the field; and where coordination is of a very low order and can be handled easily through the management process. The organization works efficiently when the business is stable and is expected to grow in a steady manner. When the business becomes competitive and develops threats to its growth, the functional structure undergoes a change. The development of people is on the specialized functions and hence   they are not equipped to handle other functions if required. The people in a functional organization develop a narrow outlook restricted to their own functions and responsibilities. The corporate culture is difficult to imbibe in a functional set- up. Most of the manufacturing, selling organisanisations in their initial period are structured on the functional lines. The government departments and agencies are organized on the functional principle.

ORGANISATIONAL BEHAVIOUR

Though an organization is structured according to the goals and objective to be achieved the actual performance is at variance for various reasons. There are some factors, beyond the control of the management which affect the performance of the organization. However there are some factors which relate to the organization (independent of the type of structure). The behavior of the organization is a result of the following factors:

1. Organizational Culture

2. Organizational Power

3. Organizational Change

4. Organizational Learning; and 5. Organizational Motivation.

A system is an assembly of elements arranged in a logical order to achieve correctives Objectives the organization is also a system of people. The individuals in the organization Are selected in terms of number quality and ability and are placed in hierarchical order to Plan and execute the business activities to achieve certain goals and objectives. This is the Simplest justification for calling the organization a system. The management theorists however have seen organization in different views and perspectives. They have identified more elements in the systems in the system besides the people. The choice of technology and structure as additional three elements of the organization system. He says that the task technology and people structure are dependent on each other and their signification cannot be ignored as elements of the system. The arrangement of task in terms of process and work design is dependent on the people. The choice of technology of handling the task is dependent on the people. You may choose the best technology and well designed task, but they have to be suited for the people. Over and above these are to be arranged in proper structure. Further a fourth Element has been added as culture. According to Leavitt an organization should be viewed as a socio- technical system consisting of people task technology culture and structure.

In view of the nature of the task the organization is supposed to carry out it has to be designed as an open system capable of adjusting itself to the changing environment. The organization continuously exchanges the information with the environment and is influenced by the changes in it.

The origination therefore has to be built in such a fashion that it adjusts with the changes in the environment and that the goals and objectives are achieved.

Hence the organization is a socio- technical system whose sub-systems are task people technology culture and structure each having its own input and output satisfying at first its own objective and eventually the corporate organization goals and objectives If the sub-systems goals and objectives are not congruent with the goals and objectives of the corporate organization poor performance resistance to change and non-attainment of corporate goals will be the consequences.

The systems and their goals are not stable. The goals change in response to the changes in the business focus the environment and in the people in the organization. A significant change calls for change in the organization structure A goals displacement is said to have occurred when the system goals significantly. Another reason for goals change is due to the. Natural process of growth and decline. This phenomenon is best described by a sigmoid or S curve. All organizations and their business go through the different phases of growth cycle in stages as Introduction Growth Maturity and Decline. Each phase generates new goals to be served if the changed or displaced goals are not reflected in the organization as a system the organization is bound to suffer from decay.

MIS: ORGANISATION

Management information systems (MIS) should be designed, viewing the organization as discussed earlier. MIS design should give due weight age to the human side of the organization and its culture. The task and technology are the physical aspects of the organization which can be ascertained very easily. But culture and people are very difficult to assess from the design point of view. The structure of the five sub-systems should be considered while designing the MIS. MIS design should give reports in line with the organization structure. This means that the main decision makers and the power centers must be recognized in the MIS. Let us discuss these aspects of the organization structure and their implications. In a tall hierarchy with a high degree of centralization, the MIS should give control information to the higher management where decision making in concentrated. If the system is structured on the functional basis where the functional head is a key decision maker and all the functions have equally important role to play, then the MIS will have a functional design with the information support to the functional head. Further, in such a set-up, an integrated MIS would be necessary, reporting the corporate status of the business to the top management.

If the organization works on a standardized system where rules, policies, systems and procedures have been laid down, then these become part of the MIS. The processing routines in the MIS incorporate these features as an integral part. This is safe as it has already been approved by the management of the organization. Along with the information, if the decision making responsibilities are also clearly defied and allocated, then the MIS can produce information reports by processing the data and summarizing the results in line with the decision maker's position in the structure. If the basic model of the organization is modified as a product or a project organization system, then the MIS should focus on the management of planning and control of the multiple functions. Besides these functions, he has to know the trouble spots and shows the interconnection with the other functions. It must summaries all information relating to the span of control of product or project manager. The MIS should be able to cater to the view of the product or the project manager and also of the top management. In the organization culture provides sufficient incentive for efficiency and results, the MIS should support this culture by providing such information which will aid the promotion of efficiency. If the culture encourages delegation of power and authority, then the MIS should incorporate the decision making rules in the system. The organization system is an open system and MIS should be so designed that it highlights the critical business, operational, technological and environmental changes to the concerned level in the organization, so that the action can be taken to correct the situation. The principle of the feed forward control should be extensively used as a design feature to provide a prior warning to the decision maker.

Since the organization system has a dynamic role to play to meet the changing needs of a business, the MIS becomes a common support system for playing the dynamic role. When an organization is moving through the business phases of introduction, growth, maturity and decline, MIS should provide an information support, relevant to that phase of the business cycle. This means the designer of MIS should foresee such requirements and make the design flexible enough to support such requirements.

The organizational learning helps to tone up the behavior of the organization. The MIS should support the learning mechanism by identifying the cause and effect in a given situation. It should keep the records of action and provide help to analyze the best action in a given situation. It should be help to build various decision models for use by the managers. The information support should be such that the group of enterprising manager should be able to improve their capabilities to perform batter. The design of the MIS, in isolation from organizational factors, is destined to fall as it just does not fit into the structure. Since organization systems in the same business differ for various reasons such as the leadership style, the management style, culture and group of people as a body and so on, it is difficult to evolve a standard model of the MIS for a business and/or an industry. MIS plays a very important role in creating organization behavior which in turn sets the goals for achievement. Technology and people decide the organization structure and style of the management.

3.3 STRATEGIC MANAGEMENT OF BUSINESS

THE CONCEPT OF CORPORATE PLANNING

A plan is a predetermined course of action to be taken in the future. It is a document containing the details of how the action will be executed and it is made against a time scale. The goals and the objective that a plan is supposed to achieve are the prerequisites of a plan. The setting of the goals and the objective is the primary task of the Management without which planning cannot begin. Planning means taking a deep look into the future and assessing the likely events in the total business environment and taking a suitable action to meet any eventuality. It further means generating the courses of action to meet the most likely eventuality. Planning is a dynamic process. As the future becomes the present reality, the course of action decided earlier may require a change. Planning, therefore, calls for a continuous assessment of the predetermined course of action versus the current requirements of the environment. The essence of planning is to see the opportunities and the threats in the future and predetermine the course of action to convert the opportunity into a business gain, and to meet the threat to avoid any business loss. Planning involves a chain of decisions, one dependent on the other, since it deals with along term period. A successful implementation of a plan means the execution of these decisions in a right manner one after another. Planning, in terms of future, can be long-range or short-range. Long-range planning is for a period of five years or more, while short-range planning is for one year at the most. The long-range planning is more concerned about the business as a whole, and deals with subject like the growth and the rate of growth, the direction of business, establishing some position in the business world by way of a corporate image, a business share and so on. On the other hand, short-range planning is more concerned with the attainment of the business results of the year. It could also be in terms of action by certain business tasks, such as lunching of a new product, starting a manufacturing facility, completing the project, achieving intermediate milestones on the way to the attainment of goals. The goals relate to long-term planning and the objective relate to the short-term planning. There is a hierarchy of objectives which together take the company to the attainment of goals. The plans, therefore, relate to the objectives when they are short-range and to goals when they are the long-range.

Long-range planning deals with resource selection, its acquisition and allocation. It deals with the technology and not with the methods or the procedures. It talks about the Strategy of achieving the goals. The right strategy improves the chance of success tremendously. At the same time, a wrong strategy means a failure in achieving the goals.

Corporate business planning deals with the corporate business goals and objectives. The business may be a manufacturing or a service; it may deal with the industry or trade; may operate in a public or a private sector; may be a national or an international business. Corporate business planning is a necessity in all cases. Though the corporate business planning deals with a company, its universe is beyond the company. The corporate business plan considers the world trends in the business, the industry, the technology, the international markets, the national priorities, the competitors, the business plans, the corporate strengths and the weaknesses for preparing a corporate plan. Planning therefore, is a complex exercise of steering the company through the complexities, the difficulties, the inhibitions and the uncertainties towards the attainment of goals and objective.

Dimensions of Planning. The corporate business plan has five dimensions.   These are time, entity, organization,elements and characteristics. Time The plan may either be long-range or short-range, but the execution of the plan is, year after year. The plan is made on a rolling basis where every year it is extended by one year, keeping the plan period as the next five years. The rolling plan provides an opportunity to correct or revise the plan in the light of any new information the planner may receive.

Entity The plan entity is the thing on which the plan is focused. The entity could be the production in terms of quantity or it could be a new product. It could be about the finance, the marketing, the capacity, the manpower or the research and development. The goals and the objectives would be stated in terms of these entities. A corporate plan may have several entities. Organisation The corporate plan ould deal with the company as a whole, but it has to be broken down for its subsidiaries, if any, such as the functional groups, the divisions, the product groups and the projects. The breaking of the corporate business plan into smaller organizational units helps to fix the responsibility for execution. The corporate plan, therefore, would be a master plan and it would comprise several subsidiary plans.

The plan is made out of several elements. The plan begins with the mission and goal which the organization would like to achieve. It may provide a vision statement for all to understand as also the purpose, focus, and direction the organization would like to move towards. It would at the outset, place certain policy statements emerging out of management.s business philosophy, culture and style of functioning followed by policy statements. Next it would declare the strategies in various business functions, which would enable the organization to achieve the business objectives and targets. It would spell out a program of execution of plan and achievements. It provides support on rules, procedures and methods of plan implementation, wherever necessary. One important element of the plan is a budget stipulated for achieving certain goals and business targets. The budgets are provided for sales, production, stocks, resources, expenses which are monitored against the time in execution period. The budgets and performance provide meaningful measure about success and failure of the plan designed to achieve certain goals.

CHARACTERISTICS

There are no definite characteristics of a corporate plan. The choice of characteristics is a matter of convenience helping to communicate to everybody concerned in the organization and for an easy understanding in execution. The features of a plan could be several and could have several parts. The plan is a confidential written document subject to charge, and known to a limited few in the organization. It is described in the quantitative and qualitative terms. The long-term plan is normally flexible while the short-term one is generally not. The plan is based on the rational assumptions about the future and gives weight age to the past achievements and corporate strength and weal messes. The typical characteristics of a corporate plan are the goals, the resources, the important milestones, the investment details and a variety of schedules.

ESSENTIALITY OF STRATEGIC PLANNING

There are some compelling reasons which force all the organizations to resort to strategic business planning. The following reasons make planning an essential management process to keep the business in a good shape and condition:

1. Market forces

2. Technological change

3. Complex diversity of business

4. Competition

5. Environment (Threats, Challenges, and Opportunities)

3.4 MARKET FORCES

It is very difficult to predict the market forces such as the demand and supply, the trend of the market growth, the consumer behavior and the choices, the emergence of new

DEVELOPMENT OF THE BUSINESS STRATEGIES

Long- range Strategic planning. Like any other business activity planning also has a process and methodology. It goes without any extra emphasis that the corporate planning is a top management responsibility. It begins with deciding the social responsibility and proceeds to spell out the business mission and goals and the strategies to achieve them. In the very beginning of the planning process it is necessary to establish and communicate to all concerned the social and economic responsibilities of the organization In order to discharge these responsibilities it is necessary to decide the purpose of the organization for which it works. Many organizations call it a mission. The mission or the aim of an organization is a broad statement of the organization.s existence which sets the direction of the organization and decides the scope and the boundaries of the business. The task after deciding the mission or the aim is to set the goal (s) for the organization. The goal is more specific and has a time scale of three to five years. It is described in the quantitative terms in the form of a ratio a norm or a level of certain business aspect such as the largest share leader in the industry dominant in certain product quality reach and distribution etc. The goals become a reference for the top management in planning the business activities. After determining the mission and the goals the next task is to set various objectives for the organization The objectives are described in terms of business results to be achieved in a short duration of a year or two The objectives are measurable and can be monitored with the help of business tools and technologies Objective may be the profitability the sales the quality standard the capacity utilization etc. When achieved the objectives will contribute to the accomplishment of the goals and subsequently the mission.

The next step in the planning process is to set targets for more detailed working and reference The objective of the business is to be translated in terms of functional and operational units for easy communication and decision making The targets may be monthly for the sales production inventory and on The targets will be the direct descendants of the objective(s). The success in achieving the goals and objective is directly dependent on the managements business strategies business is like a war where two or more business competitors are set against each other to win and are constantly in search of a strategy manner in which the resources, such as the men, the material, the money and the knowhow will be put to use over a period to achieve the goals. The resources of an organization being faced by it the game is of evolving strategies and counter strategies to win. The development of the strategy also considers the environmental factors such as the tech nology, the markets, the life style, the work culture, and the attitudes. The policies of the Government and so on a strategy helps to meet the external forces affecting the business development effectively and further ensures that the goals and the objectives are achieved. The development of the strategy considers the strength of the organization in deploying the resources and unstructured exercise of a complex nature riddled with the uncertainties (see Fig. 5.1) it sets the guidelines for use of the resources in kind and manner during the planning period.

3.5 Environment Socio- Economic Mission, Goals Purpose Factors For Strategy Formulation Strength And Weakness Of The Organisation Business Competition

ENVIRONMENT   SOCIO- ECONIMIC   MISSION, GOALS
PURPOSE

FACTORS FOR
STRATEGY FORMULATION

STRENGT AND
WEAKNESS OF
The ORGANISATION   BUSINESS   COMPETITION

FIG. 5.1

Fig. 5.1 types of strategies

A strategy means a specific decision (S) usually but not always regarding the deployment of the resources to achieve the mission or goals of the organization The right strategy beats competition and ensures the attainment of goals while a wrong strategy fails to achieve the goals Correction and improvement in case of a wrong strategy is possible at a very high cost .such a situation is described as a strategic failure.

If a strategy considers a single point of attack by a specific method .it is a mixed strategy. If a strategy acts on many fronts by different means then it is a mixed strategy the business strategy could be series of pure strategies handling several external forces simultaneously.

Hence the strategy may fall in any area of the business and may deal with any aspects of the business It could be aspects like price market product technology process quality service finance management strength and so on when the management decides to fight the external forces of a single area by choice it becomes a pure strategy if it uses or operates in more then one area then it becomes a mixed strategy. The success of an organization in spite of its strength depends on the strategic moves or planning the management pursues. The strategy may be pure or mixed It can be classified into four broad classes 1. Overall Company Strategy 2. Growth Strategy 3.Product Strategy and 4. Marketing Strategy.

These strategies are applicable to all the types of businesses and industries. Overall Company Strategy This strategy a very long- term business perspective deals with the overall strength of the entire company and evolves those policies of the business which will dominate the course of the business movement it is the most productive strategy if chosen correctly and fatal if chosen wrongfully the other strategies act under the overall company strategy. To illustrate the overall company strategy following examples is given:

1. A two wheeler manufacturing company will have a strategy of mass production and an aggressive marketing.

2. A computer manufacturer will have a strategy of adding new products every two or three years.

3. A consumer goods manufacturer will have a strategy of maximum reach to the consumer and exposure by way of a wide distribution network.

4. A company can have a strategy of remaining in the low price range and catering to the masses.

5. Another company can have a strategy of expanding very fast to capture the market.

6. A third company can have a strategy of creating a corporate brand image to build a brand loyalty e.g. Escorts , kirloskar , Godrej ,Tata , Bajaj, BHEL , MTNL. THE overall company strategy is broad- based having a far reaching effect on the different facets of business and forming the basis for generating strategies in the other areas of business.

SYSTEMS APPROACH

Systems approach to planning considers all the factors and their inter-relationship relevant to the subject. It takes a course to an analytical study of the total system, generates alternative courses of action and helps to select the best in the given circumstances. It is uses in situation of risk or uncertainty, and examines the various alternative courses of action. I help to find solutions to problems. The systems approach helps to understand the situation with clarity. It helps to sort out the factors on the principles of critical and non-critical, significant and insignificant, relevant and irrelevant, and finally controllable and uncontrollable. It tests the solutions for feasibility-technical, operational and economic. It further studies the problems of implementation of the solution.

Broadly, the systems approach has the following characteristic:

1. It uses all the areas and the branches of knowledge.

2. It follows a scientific analysis to identify the problem.

3. It uses a model of a complex situation to handle the problem.

4. It weighs cost against benefit for assessment of the alternatives.

5. It deals with the problems where time context is futuristic.

6. It considers the environment and its impact on the problem situation.

7. Every solution is tested on the grounds of rationality and feasibility, and accepts a given criterion for selection of the most preferred alternative.

8. It uses operations research models if the problem is well defined. Alternately, it uses a simulation approach to solve the problem. It uses tools such a Gantt chart, PERT/CPM, Network analysis for scheduling and coordinating the activities.

The systems approach is a way of looking at a problem in a systematic manner using the scientific methods and applying the principles of a rational decision making to solve the problem.

SENSITIVITY ANALYSIS

The sensitivity analysis helps to test the validity of the solution in variable conditions. The problem situation is handled with certain assumptions and conditions. Based on these considerations, a rational solution is found. Sensitivity analysis requires to know whether the solution will still remain valid if the assumptions changed, constraints were relaxed and new condones emerged. It helps to assess the impact of change on the solution in economic terms. If various factors are involved, the sensitivity analysis helps to assess the criticality of the factor against the impact it makes on the solution. Some factors will be highly sensitive and some will not be so. Most of the decision making problems are resolved on the principle of optimality, where you are trying to balance the two aspects of the problems, such as, inventory carrying cost versus ordering cost, waiting time cost versus idle time cost, costs, verses benefits, opportunity loss versus investment cost and so on. The sensitivity analysis helps to test the validity of the optimal solution under changed conditions.

Sensitivity analysis helps to test the solutions on the principle of utility. A solution which is economically rational and is based on sound business principles may be rejected on the principle of utility. The utility profiles of all the people in the organization are not the same. The utility profile, alternately known as a preference curve, shows the attitude and preference of the decision maker towards the gains and the losses against a time scale. The profile shows indirectly the risk-taking ability of the decision maker. It uses techniques such as the decision tree analysis, methods of discounting, payoff matrix, simulation, and the modeling.

MODELING

A model is a meaningful representation of a real situation on a mini scale, where only the significant factors of the situation are highlighted. The purpose of a model is to understand the complex situation based on only the significant factors.

There are several types of models. The model could be a physical model, like a model of a house, a park, a sports complex, etc. The model could be a scale model reducing a large body to a small one. The model could be mathematical model like break even analysis model, linear programming model, queuing model, network model, etc. Here a situation is represented in a mathematical form such as equations, matrices graphs and polynomials.

A complex situation is represented using variables, constants and parameters which play a significant role in that situation. The model is based on the relations the variables have. The relation among the variables may be linear or non-linear. The model only considers the relation of high significance. The model, when a situation is complex, tries to simplify the complexity by ignoring minor factors and emphasizing only minor important factors.

A model could be static or dynamic. The physical models are static models. Some business models like the break even analysis model, the statistical regression models and some of the O.R.programming models are static models. The static model does not change over a time period.

All the planning models and all the forecasting models are dynamic models. In a dynamic model, in addition to the variables considered, time is a dimension of the variables. The values of these variables change with the change in time. Such variables are called the stochastic variables.

A model, physical or mathematical, static or dynamic, needs to be tested for its utility or effectiveness. The model can be tested by using the control results already obtained. This would show the difference between the result given by the model and the actual result in a real life situation. If the difference is not significant, then one can say that the model represents the real situation. Once the model is proved useful, it is used for testing the various solution alternatives. The selection of a solution, from many alternative solutions, depends on the objective chosen. In a linear programming model, a solution is selected on the principle of maximization of the profit or minimization of the cost. In the queuing model a solution is selected, when the cost of the waiting time of a customer is less than the cost of the idle time of facility. The selection of a solution is based on the attainment of certain value of some aspect of the business, such as the turnover, the cost and the profit and so on.

The planning model considers those business variables which affect the business prospects and which show a significant impact on the business results. The long-range strategic models are, generally, dynamic models and the short-range management and operations models are mostly static models.

MIS: BUSINESS PLANNING

Business environment is prone to changes and this factor makes business planning very complex. Some factors such as the market forces, technological changes, complex diversity of business and competition have a significant impact on any business prospects. MIS is designed to assess and monitor these factors. The MIS design is supposed to provide some insight into these factors enabling the management to evolve some strategy to deal with them. Since these factors are a part of the environment, MIS design is required to keep a watch on environment factors and provide information to the management for a strategy formulation.

Strategy formulation is a complex task based on the strength and the weakness of the organization and the mission and goals it wishes to achieve. Strategy formulation is the responsibility of the top management and the top management relies on the MIS for information.

There are various business strategies such as overall company growth, product, market, financing and so on. MIS should provide the relevant information that would help the management in deciding the type of strategies the business needs. Every business may not require all the strategies all the time. The type of strategy is directly related to the current status of business and the goals it wishes to achieve. The MIS is supposed to provide current information on the status of the business vis-à-vis the goals. MIS is supposed to give a status with regard to whether the business is on a growth path or is stagnant or is likely to decline, and the reasons thereof. If the status of the business shows a declining trend, the strategy should be of growth. If business is losing in a particular market segment, then the strategy should be a market or a product strategy.

The continuous assessment of business progress in terms of sales, market, quality, profit and its direction becomes the major role of MIS. It should further aid the top management in strategy formulation at each stage of business. The business does not survive on a single strategy but it requires a mix of strategy operating at different levels of the management. For example, when a business is on the growth path, it would require a mix of price, product and market strategies. If a business is showing a decline, it would need a mix of price-discount, sales promotion and advertising strategies. The MIS is supposed to evaluate the strategies in terms of the impact they have on business and provide an optimum mix. The MIS is supposed to provide a strategy-pay off

matrix for such an evaluation.

In business planning, MIS should provide support to top management for focusing its attention on decision making and action. In business management, the focus shifts from one aspect to another. In the introductory phase, the focus would be on a product design and manufacturing. When the business matures and requires and requires to sustain or to consolidate, the focus would be on the post sales services and support. The MIS should provide early warning to change the focus of the management from one aspect to the other.

Evolving the strategies is not the only task the top management has to perform. It also has to provide the necessary resources to implement the strategies. The assessment of resource need, and its selection becomes a major decision for the top management. The MIS should provide information on resources, costs, quality and availability, for deciding the cost effective resource mix.

When the strategies are being implemented, it is necessary that the management gets a continuous feedback on its effectiveness in relation to the objective which they are supposed to achieve. MIS is supposed to give a critical feedback on the strategy performance. According to the nature of the feedback, the management may or may not make a change in the strategy mix, the focus and the resource allocation. MIS has certain other characteristics for the top management. It contains forecasting models to probe into the future-the business model for evaluation of the strategy performance by simulation business conditions. It contains functional models such as the

model for a new product launching, budgeting, scheduling and the models using PERT / CPM technique for planning.

MIS for the top management relies heavily on databases which are external to the organization. The management also relies heavily on the internal data which is evolved out of transaction processing. Management uses the standards, the norms, the rations and the yardsticks while planning and controlling the business activities. They are also used for designing strategies and their mix. The MIS is supposed to provide correct, precise and unbiased standards to the top management for planning.

We can summaries the role of the MIS in the top management function as follows.

MIS supports by way of information, to

1. decide the goals and objectives,

2. determine the correct status of the future business and projects,

3. provide the correct focus for the attention and action of the management,

4. evolve, decide and determine the mix of the strategies,

5. evaluate the performance and give a critical feedback on the strategic failures,

6. Provide cost-benefit evaluation to decide on the choice of resources, the mobilization of resources, and the mix of resources.

7. Generate the standards, the norms, the ratios and the yardsticks for measurement and control.

Success of a business depends on the quality of support the MIS gives to the management. The quality is assured only through an appropriate design of the MIS integrating the business plan with the MIS plan. Figure 5.3 explains the role of the MIS in strategic planning and its support in the execution and control of the management processes.

3.6 Decision Making

Decision Making Concepts

The word decision is derived from the Latin root decide, meaning to cut off. The concept of decision, therefore, is settlement, a fixed intention bringing to a conclusive result, a judgment,and a resolution. A decision is the choice out of several options made by the decision maker toachieve some objective in a given situation.

Business decisions are those, which are made in the process of conducting business to achieve its objectives in a given environment. In concept, whether we are talking about business decisions or any other decision, we assume that the decision maker is a rational person who would decide, with due regard to the rationality in decision making.

The major characteristics of the business decision making are:

(a) Sequential in nature.

(b) Exceedingly complex due to risks and trade offs.

(c) Influenced by personal vales

(d) Made in institutional settings and business environment.

The business decision making is sequential in nature. In business, the decisions are not isolated events. Each of them has a relation to some other decision or situation. The decision may appear as a .snap. decision but it is made only after a long chain of developments and a series of related earlier decision.

The decision making process is a complex process in the higher hierarchy of management. The complexity is the result of many factors, such as the inter-relationship among the experts or decision makers, a job responsibility, a question of feasibility, the codes of morals and ethics, and a probable impact on business.

The personal values of the decision maker play a major role in decision making. A decision otherwise being very sound on the business principle and economic rationality may be rejected on the basis of the personal values, which are defeated if such a decision is implemented. The culture, the discipline and the individual's commitment to the goals will decide the process and success of the decision.

Whatever may be the situation, if one analyses the factors underlying the decision making process, it would be observed that there are common characteristics in each of them. here is a definite method of arriving at a decision: and it can be put in the form of decision process model.

The decision making process requires creativity, imagination and a deep understanding of human behavior. The process covers a number of tangible and intangible factors affecting the decision process. It also requires a foresight to predict the post-decision implications and a willingness to face those implications. All decisions solve a problem but over a period of time they give rise to a number of other problems.

RATIONAL DECISION MAKING

A rational decision is the one which, effectively and efficiently, ensures the achievement of the goal for which the decision is made. If it is raining, it is rational to look for a cover so that you do not get wet. If you are in business and want to make profit, then you must produce goods and sell them at a price higher than the cost of production. In reality, there is no right or wrong decision but a rational or an irrational decision. The quality of decision making is to be judged on the rationality and not necessarily on the result it produces.

The rationality of the decision made is not the same in every situation. It will vary with the organization, the situation and the individuals view of the business situation. The rationality, therefore, is a multi-dimensional concept. For example, the business decisions in a private organization and a Public Sector Undertaking differ under the head of rationality. The reason for this difference in rationality is the different objectives of the decision makers. Any business decision if asked to be reviewed by a share-holder, a consumer, an employee, a supplier and a social scientist, will result in a different criticism with reference to their individual rationality.

This is because each one of them will view the situation in different contexts and the motive with the different objectives. Hence, whether a decision is right or wrong depends on a specific rational view. The question which further arises: Is a decision .rationales.? If it turns out to be wrong in terms of the results it produces, can we cast doubts on the rationality?

- Simon Herbert A differentiates among the types of rationality. A decision, in a given situation is:
- Objectively rational if it maximizes the value of the objective.

Subjectively rational if it maximizes the attainment of value in relation to the knowledge and awareness of the subject.

Herbert Simon A, Top Management Planning, The Macmillan Company by George A Steiner.

- Consciously rational to the extent the process of the decision making is a conscious one.
- Organizationally rational to the degree of the orientation towards the organization.
- Personally rational to the extent it achiever's an individual's personal goals.

In other words, so long as the decision maker can explain with logic and reason, the objectivity and the circumstances in which the decision is made, it can be termed as a rational decision. Whether the rationality applied is appropriate or not could be a point for debate. Gross Bertram M suggests three dimensions of rationality. First, the degree of satisfaction of human interest. Second, the degree of feasibility in achieving the objectives. Third, a consistency in decision making. If a decision maker shows a consistent behavior in the process of decision making, then one can say that he meets the test of the rationality.

3.7 Decision Methods, Tools And Procedures

Decision making is a process which the decision maker uses to arrive at a decision. The core of this process is described by Herbert Simon in a model. He describes the model in three phases as

Intelligence Design Choice

Intelligence

Raw data collected, processed and examined. Identifies a problem calling for a decision.

Design

Inventing, developing and analyzing the different decision alternatives and testing the feasibility of implementation. Assess the value of the decision outcome.

Choice

Select one alternative as a decision, based on the selection criteria.

In the intelligence phase, the MIS collects the data. The data is scanned, examined, checked and edited. Further, the data is sorted and merged with other data and computations are made, summarized and presented. In this process, the attention of the manager is drawn to all the problem situations by highlighting the significant differences between the actual and the expected, the budgeted or the targeted.

In the design phase, the manager develops a model of the problem situation on which he can generate and test the different decisions to facilitate its implementation. If the model developed is useful in generating the decision alternatives, he then further moves into phase of selection called as choice.

In the phase of choose, the manager evolves a selection criterion such as maximum profit, least cost, minimum waste, least time taken, and highest utility. The criterion is applied to the various decision alternatives and the one which satisfies the most is selected.

In these three phases, if the manager fails to reach a decision, he starts the process all over again from the intelligence phase where additional data and information is collected, the decision making model is refined, the selection criteria is changed and a decision is arrived at.

The MIS achieves this in an efficient manner without repeated use of the Simon Model again and again. An ideal MIS is supposed to make a decision for the manager.

An example of the Simon Model would illustrate further its use in the MIS. For example, a manager finds on collection and through the analysis of the data that the manufacturing plant is under-utilized and the products which are being sold are not contributing to the profits as desired.

The problem identified, therefore, is to find a product mix for the plant, whereby the plant is fully utilized within the raw material and the market constraints, and the profit is maximized. The manager having identified this as the problem of optimization, now examines the use of Linear Programming (LP) Model. The model used to evolves various decision alternatives. However, selection is made first on the basis of feasibility, and then on the basis of maximum profit.

The product mix so given is examined by the management committee. It is observed that the market constraints were not realistic in some cases, and the present plant capacity can be enhanced to improve the profit. The same model is used again to test the revised position.

Therefore, additional data is collected and an analysis is made to find out whether the average 20 per cent utilization of the capacity can be increased. A market research for some products is made and it is found that some constraints need to be removed and some reduced. Based on the revised data, LP Model is used, and the optimum solution btained.

DECISION MAKING SYSTEMS

The decision making systems can be classified in a number of ways. There are two types of systems based on the manager.s knowledge about the environment. If the manager operates in a known environment then it is a closed decision making system. The conditions of the closed decision making system are:

(a) The manager has a known set of decision alternatives and knows their outcomes fully in terms of value, if implemented.

(b) The manager has a model, a method or a rule whereby the decision alternatives can be

generated, tested, and ranked.

(c) The manager can choose one of them, based on some goal or objective.

A few examples are a product mix problem, an examination system to declare pass or fail, or an acceptance of the fixed deposits.

If the manager operates in an environment not known to him, then the decision making
system is termed as an open decision making system. The conditions of this system are:

(a) The manager does not know all the decision alternatives.

(b) The outcome of the decision is also not known fully. The knowledge of the outcome may be a probabilistic one.

(c) No method, rule or model is available to study and finalize one decision among the set of decision alternatives.

(d) It is difficult to decide an objective or a goal and, therefore, the manager resorts to that decision, where his aspirations or desires are met best.

Deciding on the possible product diversification lines, the pricing of a new product, and the plant location, are some decision making situations which fall in the category of the open decision making systems.

The MIS tries to convert every open system to a closed decision making system by providing information support for the best decision. The MIS gives the information support, whereby the manager knows more and more about the environment and the outcomes, he is able to generate the decision alternatives, test them and select one of them. A good MIS achieves this.

TYPES OF DECISIONS

The types of decisions are based on the degree of knowledge about the outcomes or the events yet to take place. If the manager has full and precise knowledge of the event or outcome which is to occur, then his problem of the decision making is not a problem. If the manager has full knowledge, then it is a situation of certainty. If he has partial knowledge or a probabilistic knowledge, then it is decision making under risk. If the manager does not have any knowledge whatsoever, then it is decision making under uncertainty.

A good MIS tries to convert a decision making situation under uncertainty to the situation

under risk and further to certainty. Decision making in the operations management, is a situation of certainty. This is mainly because the manager in this field has fairly good knowledge about the events which are to take place, has full knowledge of environment, and has predetermined decision alternatives for choice or for selection.

Decision making at the middle management level is of the risk type. This is because of the difficulty in forecasting an event with hundred per cent accuracy and the limited scope of generating the decision alternatives.

At the top management level, it is a situation of total uncertainty of account of insufficient knowledge of the external environment and the difficulty in forecasting business growth on a long-term basis.

A good MIS design gives adequate support to all the three levees of management.

Decision is made through MIS, the effectiveness of the rule can be analyzed and the rule can be revived **Nature of Decision**

Decision making is a complex situation. To resolve the complexity, the decisions are classified as programmed and non-programmed decisions.

If a decision can be based on a rule, method or even guidelines, it is called the programmed decision. If the stock level of an item is 200 numbers, then the decision to raise a purchase requisition for 400 numbers is a programmed-decision-making situation. The decision maker here is told to make a decision based on the instructions or on the rule of ordering a quantity of 400 items when its stock level reaches 200.

If such rules can be developed wherever possible, then the MIS itself can be designed to make a decision and even execute. The system in such cases plays the role of a decision maker based on a given rule or a method. Since the programmed decision is made through MIS, the effectiveness of the rule can be analyzed and the rule can be revived and modified from time to time for an improvement. The programmed decision making can be delegated to a lower level in the management cadre.

A decision which cannot be made by using a rule or a model is the non-programmed decision. Such decisions are infrequent but the stakes are usually larger. Therefore, they cannot be delegated to the lower level. The MIS in the non-programmed-decision situation can help to some extent, in identifying the problem, giving the relevant information to handle the specific decision making situation. The MIS, in other words, can develop decision support systems in the nonprogrammed-decision-making situations.

THE LAW OF REQUISITE VARIETY

In programmed decision making, it is necessary for the manager, to enumerate all the stages of the decision making situation, and provide the necessary support through rules and a formula for each one of them. The failure to provide the decision making rule, in each of them, will lead to a situation where the system will not be able to make a decision. It is, therefore, necessary to cover a requisite variety of situations with the necessary decision response.

Decision making is a complex situation. To resolve the complexity, the decisions are classified as programmed and non-programmed decisions.

If a decision can be based on a rule, method or even guidelines, it is called the programmed decision. If the stock level of an item is 200 numbers, then the decision to raise a purchase requisition for 400 numbers is a programmed-decision-making situation. The decision maker here is told to make a decision based on the instructions or on the rule of ordering a quantity of 400 items when its stock level reaches 200.

If such rules can be developed wherever possible, then the MIS itself can be designed to make a decision and even execute. The system in such cases plays the role of a decision maker based on a given rule or a method. Since the programmed and modified from time to time for an improvement. The programmed decision making can be delegated to a lower level in the management cadre.

A decision which cannot be made by using a rule or a model is the non-programmed decision. Such decisions are infrequent but the stakes are usually larger. Therefore, they cannot be delegated to the lower level. The MIS in the non-programmed-decision situation can help to some extent, in identifying the problem, giving the relevant information to handle the specific decision making situation. The MIS, in other words, can develop decision support systems in the non programmed-decision-making situations.

3.8 MIS AND DECISION MAKING CONCEPTS

It is necessary to understand the concepts of decision making as they are relevant to the design of the MIS. The Simon Model provides a conceptual design of the MIS and decision making, wherein the designer has to design the system in such a way that the problem is identified in precise terms. That means the data gathered for data analysis should be such that it provides diagnostics and also provides a path to bring the problem to surface.

In the design phase of the model, the designer is to ensure that the system provides models for decision making. These models should provide for the generation of decision alternatives, test them and pave way for the selection of one of them. In a choice phase, the designer must help to select the criteria to select one alternative amongst the many.

The concept of programmed decision making is the finest tool available to the MIS designer, whereby he can transfer decision making from a decision maker to the MIS and still retain the responsibility and accountability with the decision maker or the manager. In case of non-programmed decisions, the MIS should provide the decision support systems to handle the variability in the decision making conditions. The decision support systems provide a generalized model of decision making.

The concept of decision making systems, such as the closed and the open systems helps the designer in providing design flexibility. The closed systems are deterministic and rule based; therefore, the design needs to have limited flexibility, while in an open system, the design should be flexible to cope up with the changes required from time to time. The methods of decision making can be used directly in the MIS provided the method to be applied has been decided. A number of decision making problems call for optimization and OR models are available which can be made a part of the system. The optimization models are static and dynamic, and both can be used in the MIS. Some of the problems call for a competitive analysis, such as a payoff analysis. In these problems, the MIS can provide the analysis based on the gains, the regrets and the utility.

The concepts of the organizational and behavioral aspects of decision making provide an insight to the designer to handle the organizational culture and the constraints in the MIS. The concepts of the rationality of a business decision, the risk averseness of the managers and the tendency to avoid an uncertainty, makes the designer conscious about the human limitations, and prompts him to provide a support in the MIS to handle these limitations. The reliance on organizational learning makes the designer aware of the strength of the MIS and makes him provide the channels in the MIS to make the learning process more efficient.

The relevance of the decision making concepts is significant in the MIS design. The significance arises out of the complexity of decision making, the human factors in the decision making, the organizational and behavior aspects, and the uncertain environments.

The MIS design addressing these significant factors turns out to be the best design.

ESTABLISHING A MANAGEMENT INFORMATION SYSTEM

Information is a *critical resource* in the operation and management of organizations. Timely availability of relevant information is vital for effective performance of Managerial functions such as planning, organizing, leading, and control. An information system in an organization is like the nervous system in the human body: it is the link that connects all the organization's components together and provides for better operation and survival in a competitive environment. Indeed, today's organizations run on information.

The term *information system* usually refers to a computer-based system, one that is designed to support the operations, management, and decision functions of an organization. Information systems in organizations thus provide information support for decision makers. Information systems encompass transaction processing systems, management information systems, decision support systems, and strategic information systems.

Information consists of data that have been processed and are meaningful to a user. A system is a set of components that operate together to achieve a common purpose. Thus a management information system collects, transmits, processes, and stores data on an organization's resources, programmes, and accomplishments. The system makes possible the conversion of these data into management information for use by decision makers within the organization. A management information system, therefore, produces information that supports the management functions of an organization (Davis & Olson, 1985; Lucas, 1990; McLeod, 1995).

DATA VERSUS INFORMATION

Data refers to raw, unevaluated facts, figures, symbols, objects, events, etc. Data may be a collection of facts lying in storage, like a telephone directory or census records.

Information is data that have been put into a meaningful and useful context and communicated to a recipient who uses it to make decisions. Information involves the communication and reception of intelligence or knowledge. It appraises and notifies, surprises and stimulates, reduces uncertainty, reveals additional alternatives or helps eliminate irrelevant or poor ones, and influences individuals and stimulates them to action. An element of data may constitute information in a specific context; for example, when you want to contact your friend, his or her telephone number is a piece of information; otherwise, it is just one element of data in the telephone directory.

Computers have made the processing function much easier. Large quantities of data can be processed quickly through computers aiding in the conversion of data to information. Raw data enter the system and are transformed into the system's output, that is, information to support managers in their decision making.

CHARACTERISTICS OF INFORMATION

The characteristics of good information are relevance, timeliness, accuracy, cost-effectiveness, reliability, usability, exhaustiveness, and aggregation level. Information is relevant if it leads to improved decision making. It might also be relevant if it reaffirms a previous decision. If it does not have anything to do with your problem, it is irrelevant. For example, information about the weather conditions in Paris in January is relevant if you are considering a visit to Paris in January. Otherwise, the information is not relevant.

Timeliness refers to the currency of the information presented to the users. Currency of data or information is the time gap between the occurrence of an event in the field until its presentation to the user (decision maker). When this amount of time is very short, we describe the information system as a *real-time* system.

Accuracy is measured by comparing the data to *actual* events. The importance of accurate data varies with the type of decisions that need to be made. Payroll information must be exact. Approximations simply will not suffice. However, a general estimate of how much staff time was devoted to a particular activity may be all that is needed.

VALUE OF INFORMATION

Information has a great impact on decision making, and hence its *value is* closely tied to the decisions that result from its use. Information does not have an absolute universal value. Its value is related to those who use it, when it is used, and in what situation it is used. In this sense, information is similar to other commodities. For example, the value of a glass of water is different for someone who has lost his way in Arctic glaciers than it is to a wanderer in the Sahara Desert.

Economists distinguish value from *cost* or *price* of a commodity incurred to produce or procure the commodity. Obviously, the value of a product must be higher than its cost or price for it to be *cost-effective.*

The concept of *normative value* of information has been developed by economists and statisticians and is derived from decision theory. The basic premise of the theory is that we always have some preliminary knowledge about the occurrence of events that are relevant to our decisions. Additional information might modify our view of the occurrence probabilities and consequently change our decision and the expected payoff from the decision. The value of additional information is, hence, the difference in expected payoff obtained by reduced uncertainty about the future event.

Information supports decisions, decisions trigger actions, and actions affect the achievements or performance of the organization. If we can measure the differences in performance, we can trace the impact of information, provided that the measurements are carefully performed, the relationships among variables are well defined, and possible effects of irrelevant factors are isolated. The measured difference in performance due to informational factors is called the *realistic value* or *revealed value* of information.

For most information systems, particularly those supporting middle and top management, the resulting decisions often relate to events that are not strictly defined and involve probabilities that cannot be quantified. The decision-making process often is obscure and the outcomes are scaled by multiple and incomparable dimensions. In such cases, we may either attempt to perform a multiattribute analysis or derive an overall *subjective value*. The *subjective value* reflects people's comprehensive impression of information and the amount they are willing to pay for specific information (Ahituv, Neumann, & Riley, 1994).

INFORMATION AS AN AID TO DECISION MAKING

Simon (1977) describes the process of decision making as comprising four steps: intelligence, design, choice, and review. The *intelligence* stage encompasses collection, classification, processing, and presentation of data relating to the organization and its environment. This is necessary to identify situations calling for decision. During the *decision* stage, the decision maker outlines alternative solutions, each of which involves a set of actions to be taken. The data gathered during the intelligence stage are now used by statistical and other models to forecast possible outcomes for each alternative. Each alternative can also be examined for technological, behavioural, and economic feasibility. In the *choice* stage, the decision maker must select one of the alternatives that will best contribute to the goals of the organization. Past choices can be subjected to *review* during implementation and monitoring to enable the manager to learn from mistakes. Information plays an important role in all four stages of the decision process. Figure 1 indicates the information requirement at each stage, along with the functions performed at each stage and the feedback loops between stages.

CLASSIFICATION OF MANAGEMENT INFORMATION SYSTEMS

There are various types of management information systems. Mason and Swanson (1981) describe four categories of management information systems: (1) databank information system, (2) predictive information system, (3) decision-making information system, and (4) decision-taking information system. The classification is based on the level of support that the information system provides in the process of decision making.:

Databank *Information System.* The responsibility of this information system is to observe, classify, and store any item of data which might be potentially useful to the decision making.

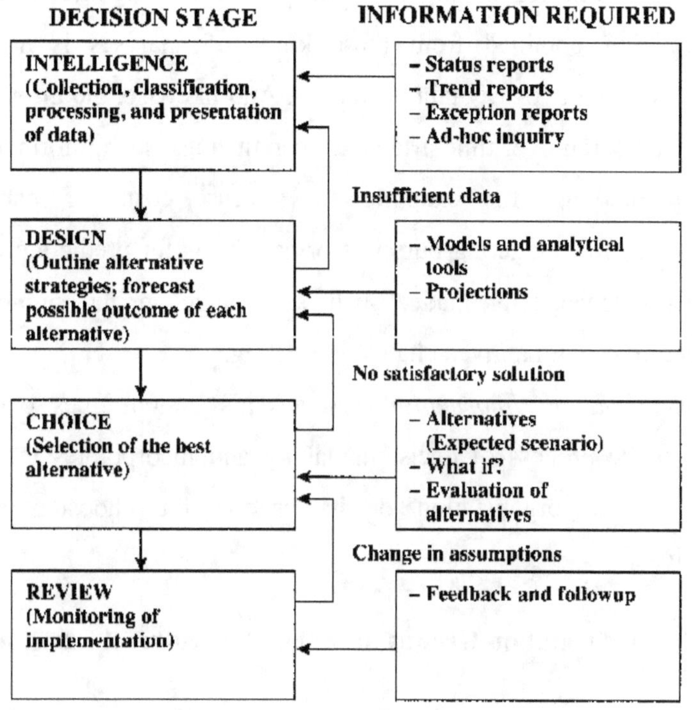

Each of these databases can be summarized and converted to single tabular presentations of information of interest to management. When information from two or more time periods is compared, trends can be observed.

Predictive Information System. This system moves beyond pure data collection and the determination of trends over time. Predictive information systems provide for the drawing of inferences and predictions that are relevant to decision making. If data from the above examples were to be used in this way, it is possible to obtain information useful for making predictions or for drawing inferences

Information obtained from these kinds of analyses is normally summarized in a two-way tabular format. And likewise, the information often is compared over time. Managers can then use such information to make predictions, for example to forecast costs of particular undertakings for budgeting purposes or as a basis for predicting results if a given change is made, such as change in the number of demonstrations with a given change in staffing.

Decision-*Making Information System.* This system goes one step further in the process of decision making and incorporates the value system of the organization or its criteria for choosing among alternatives.

Table. Information Groups in India's Agricultural Extension System.

Levels	Groups	Types of Information Needed
Central	Extension commissioner, joint commissioners, directors, joint directors, etc. of the directorate of extension, ministry of agriculture	(1) Information on human resources, plans, and budgets for various extension of services (2) Statewide monitoring and evaluation of activities

		completed
State	Director of agriculture, additional director, joint directors, etc. of the state department of agriculture	(1) Districtwide information on extension programmes, activities, expenditures, etc (2) Research-extension linkages and coordination with other allied departments such as animal husbandry and horticulture
District	District agricultural officers (DAOs)	(1) Information on extension resources and constraints at subdivision and block levels (2) Training requirements of staff at subdivision and block levels
Subdivision	Subdivisional agricultural officers	(1) Field demonstration programmes, activities planned and implemented by subject-matter specialists (SMSs) (zone) at the block level (2) Technical programme and constraints identified at the block level

| Block (county) | Agricultural officers | extension | (1) Performance of VEWs in terms of achievements in extension activities
 (2) Field-level problem of assessment of beneficiaries' response to various extension programmes |

Decision-Taking Information System. Examples of decision-taking information systems are not usually found in an extension organization. This is a decision system in which the information system and the decision maker are one and the same. Management is so confident in the assumptions incorporated in the system that it basically relegates its power to initiate action to the system itself. Airplanes carry automatic pilot systems, which are an example of a decision-taking system. Once activated, the system itself keeps the plane on course and at the proper speed and altitude (according to parameters determined by the pilot). Another example of decision-taking information systems is found in modem factory production. In automobile production, continuous inventories of parts are maintained by computer as cars move down an assembly line. Orders are placed automatically by the computer when additional parts are needed. This is done without the intervention of a manager.

The choice of an appropriate management information system (MIS) category primarily depends on the nature of the decisions it supports. While unstructured decisions may use MIS-category (I), the highly structured ones, such as production schedules in an industry, may use MIS-category (iv). Further, Banerjee and Sachdeva (1995) observe that "as the deep structure of the decision problem becomes more and more understood, we may move to higher level of MIS i.e., from MIS-category (I) to MIS-category (ii); and MIS-category (ii) to MIS-category (iii); and so on."

ROLE OF MIS IN THE MANAGEMENT OF AGRICULTURAL EXTENSION PROGRAMMES

The main purpose of management information systems is to provide management information to decision makers at various levels in the organization. Specifically, in an agricultural extension organization, MIS is needed:

1. To plan the most effective allocation of resources, for example, the allocation of extension personnel under a T & V extension system, the need for communications and training equipment and facilities, mobility, the amounts of required operational resources

2. To choose between alternative courses of action, whether to conduct a study on the impact of the T & V system with the resources on hand or hire an expert to investigate

3. To control day-to-day operations, for example, comparing the actual results achieved and those planned under the T & V system.

3.9 NEED FOR AUTOMATION

An automated MIS system contains data just as a manual system does. It receives input, processes input, and delivers the processed input as output. Some input devices allow direct human-machine communication, while others require data to be recorded on an input medium such as a magnetizable material (specially coated plastic flexible or *floppy*disks and magnetic tapes). The keyboard of a workstation connected directly to a computer is an example of a direct input device. Use of automation makes it possible to store immense quantities of information, to avoid many of the errors that find their way into manual records, and to make calculations and comparisons that would be practically impossible in a manual system.

3.10 ORGANIZATION OF A DATABASE

Data are usually generated at the field level through transaction-processing systems, but once the data are captured, any echelon along the organizational hierarchy may use them, provided that information requirements have been well defined, appropriate programmes have been implemented, and a means has been arranged for the sharing of the data. This would imply that the same data can be used by different sets of programmes; hence we distinguish between the database (a set of data) and the applications (a set of programmes). In a decision support system (DSS), this set of programmes is the *model base* (Keen & Morton, 1978).

The term *database* may refer to any collection of data that might serve an organizational unit. A database on a given subject is a collection of data on that subject that observes three criteria: comprehensiveness (completeness), nonredundancy, and appropriate structure. Comprehensiveness means that all the data about the subject are actually present in the database. Nonredundancy means that each individual piece of data exists only once in the database. Appropriate structure means that the data are stored in such a way as to minimize the cost of expected processing and storage (Awad & Gotterer, 1992).

The idea of a large corporate database that can be flexibly shared by several applications or model bases has been realized by means of software packages specially devised to perform such tasks. These packages, called *database management systems* (DBMSs), are available in the market under different trade names such as ORACLE, SYBASE, INGRES, FOXBASE, and dBASE.

NETWORKING AND INTERACTIVE PROCESSING

The two principal blocks that facilitate development and use of MIS are DBMS and telecommunications. The former makes data integration possible, while the latter brings information closer to the end users, who constitute nodes in a telecommunication network. The notion of telecommunications implies that some geographical distance exists between the computer site and the users' locations and that data are electronically transmitted between them. Remote applications may be executed between two floors in the same building, two offices in the same city, two offices on the same continent, or two places on opposite sides of the globe (Martin, 1990).

System alternatives and evaluation: Centralization versus decentralization

A completely centralized information system handles all processing at a single computer site, maintains a single central database, has centralized development of applications, provides central technical services, sets development priorities centrally, and allocates computer resources centrally. The system's remote users are served by transporting input and output data physically or electronically.

A completely decentralized system may have no central control of system development, no communication links among autonomous computing units, and stand-alone processors and databases at various sites. Each unit funds its own information-processing activities and is totally responsible for all development and operation.

An advantage of centralized information systems is that they provide for standardization in the collection of data and the release of information. There also are some *economies of scale. A* centralized system reduces the need for multiple hardware, software, space, personnel, and databases. It may be possible to recruit more qualified personnel in a central facility.

Observations indicate that user motivation and satisfaction are increased under a decentralized environment. This is attained because users feel more involved and more responsible, systems are better customized to their specific needs, and they usually get better response time in routine operations as well as in requests for changes.

It is likely that for national agricultural extension systems, neither a completely centralized nor a completely decentralized system is desirable. While it may be useful to decentralize hardware and software resources at different locations, the development of applications and provision of technical services may better be centralized.

END-USER COMPUTING

The widespread use of personal computers and computer-based workstations has brought with it the age of end-user computing. End-user computing is a generic term for any information-processing activity performed by direct end users who actually use terminals or microcomputers to access data and programmes. The manager as end user may be provided with powerful software (like DBMS) for accessing data, developing models, and performing information processing directly. This has brought computing directly under the control of the end users and eliminates their dependence on the information systems specialist and the rigidities of predesigned procedures. They may now make ad hoc queries of information and analyse it in various ways. They may write programmes, or may often use ready-made programmes stored in the computer, using the computing power of a local PC or the mainframe to which it is connected.

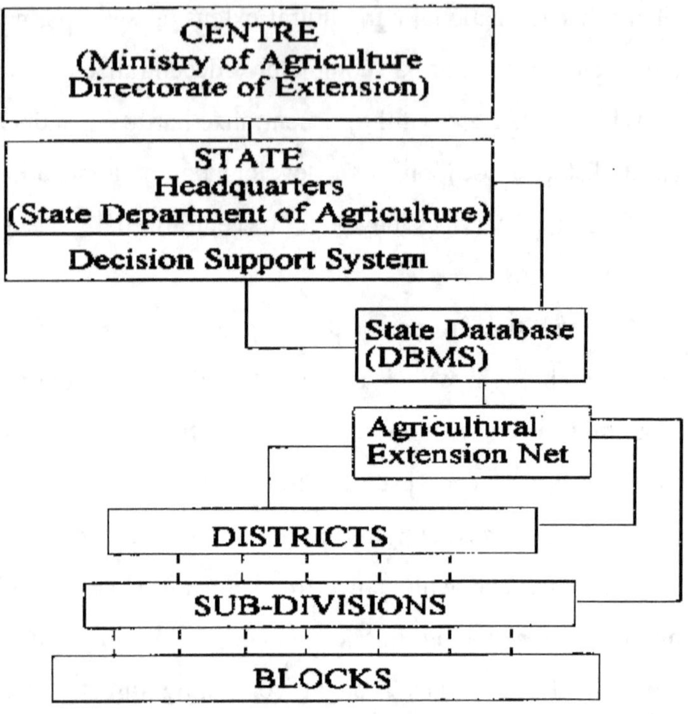

Figure 2. A typical MIS for a national extension system

ILLUSTRATIVE COMPUTER-BASED MIS

A national agricultural extension system is a nationwide system managed by the national government. In India, agriculture is a state subject under the division of powers between the national and the state levels. Nevertheless, the national government supplements the financial resources of the states and provides coordination at the national level. The state's administrative machinery is divided into districts, districts into subdivisions, subdivisions into blocks. A block is a group of villages and the basic unit for the administration of an agricultural extension programme. Data collected at the block level need to be integrated at higher administrative levels to provide an integrated view at the district and state levels to support planning, monitoring, and decision making.

Keeping in view the requirements of the extension system and the budget constraints of the states, a typical design of the computer-based MIS is shown in Figure 2.

However, the actual design may vary with the size of the state and other considerations. An integrated database for the entire state may be supported by a mainframe/minicomputer at the state headquarters. Suitable programmes for the analysis of data may be designed to provide an interactive decision support system at the state level. Each district and subdivision may be provided with a mini/micro computer, depending on the volume of data to be handled. The computers in the districts and subdivisions may be networked with the state computer. The local data may be stored and processed in the district/subdivision, and the shared data with appropriate level of aggregation may be transmitted to the state headquarters to update the integrated database. The districts and subdivisions would have direct access to the integrated database with proper authorizations assigned to them through their passwords. The blocks may have only the input-output terminals connected to the subdivision computer to feed data to the subdivision and make on-line inquiries as and when necessary.

3.11 SUMMARY

In this chapter, we have defined and described the basic concepts of a management information system. The characteristics of good information, namely, relevance, timeliness, accuracy, cost-effectiveness, reliability, usability, exhaustiveness, and aggregation level, have been described. The role of information systems in the process of decision making and the value of information have been explained. Four types of MIS, namely, databank information system, predictive information system, decision-making information system, and decisiontaking information system, have been presented.

Basic computer concepts have been explained. The advantages and disadvantages of centralized versus decentralized systems have been examined. The need for organizing databases and their integration and the need for programmes for decision analysis to evolve a decision support system have been explained. An assessment of hardware, software, and networking requirements for a typical computer-based MIS for a national agricultural extension system have been illustrated.

Unit IV

The Role of Management Information System (MIS) and Decision Support System (DSS) for Manager's Decision Making Process

4.1 MIS AND THE ROLE OF DSS

The Decision Support System (DSS) is a special class of system which is used as a support in decision making. Many of the decision making situations, at all levels of management, are such that its occurrence is infrequent but the methodology of decision making is known. Some of the methods are proven and are widely used. Such applications are separated and are packed in the DSS.

These systems use data from the general MIS and they are used by a manager or a decision maker for decision support. The basic characteristic of the decision support system is that it is based on some tool, technique or model. These systems are used sometimes for resting new alternatives, training and learning. They are also used for sensitizing the various parameters of the model.

The DSS could be an internal part of the MIS. When the decision making need is in real time dynamic mode, all such systems are designed to read, measure, monitor, evaluate, analyze and act as per the decision guidance embedded in the system. For example, in a simple case of order processing, the embedded DSS will accept or reject the order based on the CRISIL, credit rating, availability of stock and so on. If the order is accepted, the order acceptance is generated and the dispatch is scheduled for the ordered quantity. The DSS, in all such cases, uses the data already present in the system and gets it activated for action as per the guidelines.

The MIS designer has to look for all such situations and design the DSS for integration in the system. The MIS would become more useful if the decision making is made person-independent and executed with well-designed DSS. All such embedded systems cover the normal variety of decision situations. If anything outside the considered variety crops up, DSS will bring to the notice of the decision makers that action is called for in the situation.

When the decision situation requires multidimensional analysis using the internal and external data, then such decision support systems are kept out of the main MIS design scope. Most of this situation calls for the use of models and the nature of decision is strategic, calling for planned activity.

Decisions like a new product launch, price revision, appointing new dealers, change of product design or change in the manufacturing process are strategic decisions which require critical analysis of data, careful evaluation of various alternatives and selecting one of them for implementation on the given criteria.

The decision support system plays a dominant role in the management.

In today's business world, there are varieties of information systems such as TPS, DAS, KWS, MIS, DSS, ES, CSCWS, GDSS and ESS. Each plays a different role in organizational hierarchy and decision making process. In this article the authors have selected two main information systems, namely, MIS and DSS. After discussing the decision making process based on each concept, its characteristics, relations, connections of each concept to decision-making process have been determined. At the same time, different models and figures are presented to enrich the discussion and to highlight precisely the status of each MIS and DSS information system in organizational decision making.

Keywords: Management information system, Decision support system, Managers, Decision making process

4.2 INTRODUCTION

For the last twenty years, different kinds of information systems are developed for different purposes, depending on the need of the business. Transaction Process Systems (TPS) function in operational level to process large amount of data for routine business transactions of the organization, Office Automation Systems (OAS) support data workers and Knowledge Work Systems (KWS) support professional workers. Higher-level systems include Management Information Systems (MIS) and Decision Support Systems (DSS). Expert System (ES) applies the expertise of decision makers to solve specific, unstructured problems. At the strategic level of management, there is Executive Support Systems (ESS). Group Decision Support Systems (GDSS) and the more generally described Computer Supported Collaborative Work (CSCW) systems aid group level decision making of a semi structured or unstructured decision.

In the present article the authors discuss two kinds of information systems, namely, MIS, and DSS, and then their characteristics, interrelationship and their relations with decision-making process in an organization.

4.3 DECISION MAKING PROCESS

In the 1950s, Herbert Simon and James March for the first time introduced a different decision making framework for understanding organizational behavior. Although they labored on the bureaucratic model by emphasizing on individual work in rational organizations and thus behaving rationally, their model added a new dimension: The idea that a human being's rationality is limited. By offering a more realistic alternative to classical assumption of rational in decision-making, this model supported the behavioral view of individual and organizational functioning. The model suggested that when an individual makes decision, he examines a limited set of possible alternatives rather than all available options. "He accepts satisfactory or good enough" choices, rather than insist on optimal choices. He makes choices that are good enough because he does not search until he finds perfect solution to a problem (Gordon, 1993). Simon divided kinds of decisions into two basic types: programmed and non programmed decisions.

Programmed decisions are routine and repetitive decisions, and the organization typically develops specific ways to handle them. For this kind of routine repetitive decisions, standard arrangement decisions are typically made according to established management guidelines.

Non-programmed decisions, in contrast, are typically one-shot decisions that are usually less structured than programmed decisions

4.4 MIS Characteristics

In general, management information systems have a number of characteristic, which include the following:

1. Report with fixed and standard formation. For example scheduled reports for inventory control may contain the same type of information placed in the same location on the reports.

2. Have report developed and implemented using information system personnel, including systems analysts and computer programmer. Typically analysts and programmers are involved in developing and implementing MIS reports. User is normally involved in the design of the reports, but they are not typically involved in writing the computer programs to produce them.

3. Require formal request from user. Because information systems personnel typically develop and implement MIS reports, a formal request to the information systems department for report is usually required.

4. Produce scheduled and demand reports. The major type of reports produced by an MIS is scheduled; demand reports (Stair, 1992).

5. External data is not captured by the organization but is used by the MIS. (i.e., customer, supplier and competitor information).

THE ROLE OF MIS IN DECISION MAKING PROCESS

The MIS and its organizational subsystems contribute to decision making process in many basic ways. Nowadays, some of the organizations use MIS to assist managers for decision making. For example, to assist decision-makers in extracting synthesized information from a massive database such as the Current Public Transport Record (CPTR) of Durban (CPTR), the Durban Unicity Council decided to make use of a Public

Transport Management Information System (PTMIS) developed by Stewart Scott. This system is for use by transport planners and managers (Louw et al, 2001).

Power (2002) has stated that making decisions is an important part of working in business environment. Companies often make decisions regarding operational improvements or selecting new business opportunities for maximizing the company's profit. Companies develop a decision-making process based on individuals responsible for making decisions and the scope of the company's business operations. A useful tool for making business decisions is a management information system (MIS). Historically, the MIS was a manual process used to gather information and funnel it to individuals responsible for making decisions.

4.5 ORGANIZATION–WIDE INFORMATION RESOURCE

The MIS is an organization – wide effort to provide decision making process information. The system is a formal commitment by executive to make the computer available to all managers. The MIS sets the stage for accomplishments in the other area, which is DSS, the virtual office and knowledge based systems. Situation analysis, problem identification and understanding The main idea behind the MIS is to keep a continuous supply of information flowing to the management.

Afterward by data and information gathered from MIS system, make decisions.

Decision Support System (DSS) A decision support system or DSS is a computer based system intended for use by a particular manager or usually a group of managers at any organizational level in making a decision in the process of solving a semi structured decision (Figure 7). The DSS produces output in the form of periodic or special report or the results of mathematical simulations (Raymond, 1990). It is difficult to pinpoint that are completely structured or unstructured. The vast majorities are semi structured. This means that the DSS is aimed at the area where most semi structured decision is needed to be made.

4.6 A DSS MODEL

A DSS model includes four parts as follows (Raymond, 1998).

- Data base produces both internal and environmental data, which are stored in the database.
- Report writing software produces both periodic and special reports. Periodical reports are prepared according to a schedule and typically they are produced by software, which is coded in a procedural language such as COBOL or PL/I. The special report is prepared in response to unanticipated information need and

takes form of database by users who use the query language of a DBMS or fourth generation language.

- Mathematical model produces information as a result of either simulation that involves one or more components of the physical system of the firm or facts of its operations. Mathematical models can be written in any procedural programming language. However, special model languages make this task easier and have the potential of doing a better job.

- Groupware enables multiple decision makers, working together as a group, to reach solutions. In this particular situation, the term GDSS, or a group decision support system is used. Perhaps the decision makers represent a committee or a project team. The group members communicate with one another both, directly and by means of the group ware.

The reports writing software and mathematical model have always been regarded as necessary DSS ingredients.

As the DSS concept was broadened to provide support to two or more decision maker working together as a team or committee, the idea of special group oriented software or groupware, became a reality.

4.7 DSS Characteristics

Decision support system has a number of characteristics, which include following:

- DSS provide support for decision maker mainly in semi structured and unstructured situations by bringing together human judgment and computerized information. Such problem cannot be solved (cannot be solved conveniently) by other computerized systems, such as MIS.

- DSS attempts to improve the effectiveness of decision-making (accuracy, timeliness, quality) rather than its efficiency (cost of making the decision, including the charges for computer time) (Davis & Olson, - DSS provides support to individuals as well as to groups. Many organizational problems involve group decision-making. The less structured problem frequently requires the involvement of several individuals from different departments and organizational levels.

- Advanced DSS are equipped by a knowledge component, which enables the efficient and effective solution of very difficult problems (Turban & Aronson, 1998).

- A DSS can handle large amount of data for instance advanced database management package have allowed decision makers, to search database for information. A DSS can also solve problems where a small amount of data is required.

- A DSS can be developed using a modular approach. With this approach, separate functions of the DSS are placed in separate modules - program or subroutines-allowing efficient testing and implement of systems. It also allows various modules to be used for multiple purposes in different systems.

- A DSS has a graphical orientation. It has often been said that a picture is worth a thousand words.

Today's decision support systems can help managers make attractive, informative graphical presentations on computer screens and on printed documents. Many of today's software packages can produce line drawing, pie chart, trend line and more. This graphical orientation can help decision makers a better understanding of the true situation in a given market place.

- A DSS support optimization and heuristic approach. For smaller problems, DSS has the ability to find the best (optimal) situation. For more complex problems, heuristics are used. With heuristic, the computer system can determine a very good-but not necessarily the best- solution. This approach gives the decision maker a great deal of flexibility in getting computer support for decision making activities.

- A DSS can perform "what – if" and goal – seeking analysis. "What – if "analysis is the process of making hypothetical change to problem data and observing impact of the results. In with" what – if "analysis, a manager can make changes to problem data (the number of automobiles for next month) and immediately see the impact on the requirement for subassemblies (engines, windows, etc.) (Stair, 1992).

4.8 THE ROLE OF THE DSS IN THE PROCESS OF DECISION MAKING

Previously it was mentioned that the MIS is best suited in identifying problems and helping managers understanding them to make suitable and correct decisions, but the main weakness of MIS is that it is not aimed at the specific need of the individual and group decision makers.

Very often the MIS does not provide exactly the information that is needed to solve problems for individual and group decision making. DSS is tailored to the specific need of the individual and group managers. Therefore, the DSS can extend this support through the remaining steps (in objective and criteria setting, alternative search, alternative evaluation, making the decision and decision review) of the decision making. Finally DSS has more roles in decision-making and problem solving than MIS (Raymond, 1998). The other researches such as the following confirm this idea:

Uma (2009) has stated that a Decision Support System is an integrated set of computer tools allowing a decision maker to interact directly with computer to retrieve information useful in making semi structured and unstructured decisions. Example of this decisions include such things as merger and acquisition decisions, plant expansion, new product decisions portfolio management and marketing decisions.

Nokhbatolfoghahaayee et al (2010) have introduced a fuzzy decision support system FDSS) with a new decision making structure, which can be applied to manage the crisis conditions in any large scale systems with many parameters. After receiving both functional variables of the system and fault signals, the FDSS makes proper decisions to make up and repair the distorted situation and the affected elements of the network according to its data base established through experience gathered from expert managers and decision models properly developed. These decisions are expressed in the form of some scenarios with different desirability degrees, which are determined by some properly developed fuzzy multi-criteria decision making methods, helping the manager choose the best one according to his discretion.

Alonso et al (2010) have presented an implemented web based consensus support system that is able to help, or even replace, the moderator in a consensus process where experts are allowed to provide their preferences using one of many types (fuzzy, linguistic and multi-granular linguistic) of incomplete preference relations.

These studies show the important and role of MIS during managers' decision making process.

4.9 DISCUSSION

Managers in all levels of organization hierarchy need precise and suitable data and information to make decisions that increase organizational performance. Such concept suggests an informational need of supervisory level is different from top level. At the same time the type of information also at each level is different. At lower level, supervisors need defined, clear, precise, quantifiable and internal organizational information but at the top level a manager needs undefined, future oriented, infrequent, summarized, relatively, non quantifiable and mostly external information. Quantifiable information could be gathered from external environment if suitable. Management Information Systems are placed in organizational information system such as CSCWS, GDSS and ESS. And some of environment elements such a socio-cultural factors like birth rate, population rate, competitor's share of market and so on could be quantifiable data and be considered and used it the process of top level management decision making process.

In general, different kinds of data and information are suitable for decision-making in different levels of organizational hierarchy and require different information system to be placed. Such system could have explicit effect on each step of decision process in solving problems. At the same time each information system cannot fulfill complete information needs of each level, but rather different information systems if integrated in different levels could satisfy information needs of a level and at the same time fulfill part of information needs of other levels. For example TPS fulfills the lower level needs of an organization but MIS furnishes data and information for lower and middle level management needs. On the other hand, DSS furnishes information for middle level and higher level of organizational hierarchy and ES fulfills only higher level managerial needs. Clearly by segregating each IS, its particular function could be recognized and it's overlapping distinguished..

The data from EDP system transfers to DBMS and helps managers to make programmed and non-programmed decisions . The flow of data after moving from EDP system to DBMS will move from MIS level to DSS and at the same time part of processed data will be restored in EDP system.

4.10 CONCLUSION

Apart from variety of information system in business world, MIS and DSS were the main concern of present article. It was found that MIS is best suited to identify problems and help management to understand them to make suitable decisions. At the same time, MIS is not aimed to help particular and specific need of the individual and group decision making. On the other hand DSS are tailored to the specific need of individual and group managers. Therefore, it could be concluded, that DSS can extend its support to the same steps of decision making process and has more roles in decision-making and problem solving than MIS. Due to some practical limitations, may be some of steps of decision making process to be chosen and the others to be removed. It is important to consider which ones are preferred to the other ones. In future works can study on the role of other information systems for managers' decision making and comparative it to DSS and MIS.

4.11 BENIFITS

The following are some of the benefits that can be attained for different types of MISs

- Companies are able to highlight their strengths and weaknesses due to the presence of revenue reports, employees' performance record etc. The identification of these aspects can help the company improve their business processes and operations.
- Giving an overall picture of the company and acting as a communication and planning tool.

- The availability of customer data and feedback can help the company to align their business processes according to the needs of the customers. The effective management of customer data can help the company to perform direct marketing and promotion activities.

- MISs can help a company gain a competitive advantage. Competitive advantage is a firm's ability to do something better, faster, cheaper, or uniquely, when compared with rival firms in the market.

4.12 ENTERPRISE APPLICATION

- *Enterprise systems*—also known as *enterprise resource planning (ERP)* systems—provide integrated software modules and a unified database that personnel use to plan, manage, and control core business processes across multiple locations. Modules of ERP systems may include finance, accounting, marketing, human resources, production, inventory management, and distribution.

- *Supply chain management (SCM)* systems enable more efficient management of the supply chain by integrating the links in a supply chain. This may include suppliers, manufacturers, wholesalers, retailers, and final customers.

- *Customer relationship management (CRM)* systems help businesses manage relationships with potential and current customers and business partners across marketing, sales, and service.

- *Knowledge management system (KMS)* helps organizations facilitate the collection, recording, organization, retrieval, and dissemination of knowledge. This may include documents, accounting records, unrecorded procedures, practices, and skills. Knowledge management (KM) as a system covers the process of knowledge creation and acquisition from internal processes and the external world. The collected knowledge is incorporated in organizational policies and procedures, and then disseminated to the stakeholders.

Unit V

"The actions that are taken to create an information system that solves an organizational problem are called system development".[14] These include system analysis, system design, computer programming/implementation, testing, conversion, production and finally maintenance. These actions usually take place in that specified order but some may need to repeat or be accomplished concurrently.

Conversion is the process of changing or converting the old system into the new. This can be done in three basic ways, though newer methods (prototyping, Extreme Programming, JAD, etc.) are replacing these traditional conversion methods in many cases:

- Direct cut – The new system replaces the old at an appointed time.

- Pilot study –– Introducing the new system to a small portion of the operation to see how it fares. If good then the new system expands to the rest of the company.

Phased approach – New system is introduced in stages.

5.1 Summary Of Information Concepts And Their Implications

Understanding of information concepts is very important and relevant to the system designer and the information user. The concepts are summarized as follows.

Filtering

The system designer should provide an appropriate filtering mechanism so that the information is not suppressed and relates to the frame of reference of the user. Care should be taken in the process that certain valid information does not get blocked or over emphasized. A filtering process is used to select and suppress the information.

SIMON MODEL AND ITS APPLICATION

The designer should attempt to provide such information that it clearly defines the problem space and also takes cognizance of the user.s knowledge. The design of the system should be such that an appropriate mix of these two sources should yield a decision, leading to a solution of the problem.

CODES AND REPRESENTATION

The system designer should evolve such coding system that is easy for the users of the code to interpret. Secondly, the designer should report the data in such a manner that the user can grasp it quickly.

HIGHLIGHTING

The designer should the information in such a way that the significant differences between the targets and the achievements, the standards and the performance, the budgets and the actual, are highlighted, so that they become easily noticeable by the user without search.

STATISTICAL ANALYSIS

The designer should provide the information in such a way that the information not only represents something meaningfully but also aids in the statistical analysis by the user. The information should provide the additional results such as variance, correlation, coefficients, and futuristic estimates and give a measure of statistical significance for the user to consider while decision making.

5.2 DEVELOPMENT OF LONG RANGE PLANS OF THE MIS

Any kind of business activity calls for long range plans for success, the same being true for MIS. The plan for development and its implementation is a basic necessity for MIS. In MIS the information is recognized as a major resource like capital, time and capacity. And if this resource is to be managed well, it calls upon the management to plan for it and control it for the appropriate use in the organization. Most of the organizations do not recognize 'Information' as a resource. They have looked at information as one of the many necessities for conducting the business activity. Hence, due regard is often not given for its planned development and use. Many organizations have spent financial resources on computers purely to expedite the activity of data collection and processing.

Many organizations have purchased computers for data processing and for meeting the statutory requirements of filing the returns and reports to the Government. Computers are used mainly for computing and accounting the business transactions and have not been considered as a tool for information processing.

The organizations have invested in computers and expanded its use by adding more or bigger computers to take care of the numerous transactions in the business. In this approach the information processing function of the computers in the organization never got it s due regard as an important asset to the organization. In fact, this function is misinterpreted as data processing for expeditious generation of reports and returns, and not as information processing for management action and decisions.

However, the scheme has been changing since late eighties when the computers became more versatile, in the function of Storage, Communication, Intelligence and Language. The computer technology is so advanced that the barriers of storage, distance, understanding of language and speed are broken.

With the advancement of computer technology, it is now possible to recognize information as valuable resources like money and capacity.

In short, we need a Management Information System flexible enough to deal with the changing information needs of the organization. It should be conceived as an open system continuously interacting with the business environment with a built-in mechanism to provide the desired information as per the new requirements of the management. The designing of such as open system is a complex task. It can be achieved only if the MIS is planned, keeping in view, the plan of the business management of the organization.

The plan of MIS is concurrent to the business plan of the organization. The information needs for the implementation of the business plan should find place in the MIS. To ensure such an alignment possibility, it is necessary that the business plan – strategic or otherwise, states the information needs. The information needs are the traced to the source data and the systems in the organization which generate such a data. The plan of development of the MIS is linked with the steps of the implementation in a business development plan. The system of information generation is so planned that strategic information is provided for the strategic planning, control information is provided for a short term planning and execution.

Any kind of business activity calls for long range plans for success, the same being true for MIS. The plan for development and its implementation is a basic necessity for MIS. In MIS the information is recognized as a major resource like capital, time and capacity. And if this resource is to be managed well, it calls upon the management to plan for it and control it for the appropriate use in the organization. Most of the organization does not recognize .Information. as a resource. They have looked at information as one of the many necessities for conducting the business activity. Hence, due regard is often not given for its planned development and use. Many organizations have spent financial resources on computers purely to expedite the activity of data collection and processing. Many organizations have purchased computers data processing and for meeting the statutory requirement of filing the return and reports to the Government. Computers
are used mainly for computing and accounting the business transactions and have not been considered as a tool for information processing.

The organizations have invested in computers and expanded its use by adding more or bigger computers to take care of the numerous transactions in the business. In this approach, the information processing function of the computers in the organization never got its due regard as an important asset to the organization. In fact, this function is misinterpreted as data processing for expeditious generation of reports and returns, and not as information processing for management actions and decisions.

However, the scene has been changing since late eighties when the computers became more versatile, in the function of Storage, Communications, Intelligence and Language. The computer technology is so advanced that the barriers of storage, distance, understanding of language and speed are broken.

The computers have become user-friendly. They can communicate to any distance and share data, information and physical resources of other computers. Computers can now be used as a tool for information processing and communication. It can be used for storing large database or knowledge base. It can be used for knowing the current status of any aspect of the business due to its on-line real time processing capability.

USEFULNESS

In short, we need a Management Information System flexible enough to deal with the changing information needs of the organization. It should be conceived as an open system continuously interacting with the business environment with a built-in mechanism to provide the desired information as per the new requirements of the management. The designing of such an open system is a complex task. It can be achieved only if the MIS is planned, keeping in view, the plan of the business management of the organization.

The plan of MIS is concurrent to the business plan of the organization.

The information needs for the implementation of the business plan should find place in the MIS. To ensure such an alignment possibility, it is necessary that the business plan strategic or otherwise, states the information needs. The information needs are then traced to the source data and the systems in the organization which generate such a data. The plan of development of the MIS is linked with the steps of the implementation in a business development plan. The system of information generation is so planned that strategic information is provided for the strategic planning, control information is provided for a short term planning and execution. The details of information are provided to the operations management to assess the status of an activity and to find ways to make up, if necessary. Once the management needs are translated into information needs, it is left for the designer to evolve a plan of development and implementation.

CONTENTS OF THE MIS PLAN

A long range MIS plan provides direction for the development of the systems, and provides a basis for achieving the specific targets or tasks against a time frame. The plan would have the following contents which will be dealt by the designer under a support from the top management. shows equivalence of Business Plan and MIS plan.

5.3 MIS Plan is Linked to the Business Plan Goals and Objectives

It is necessary to develop the goals and objectives for the MIS which will support the business goals. The MIS goals and objectives will consider management philosophy, policy constraints, business risks, internal and external environment of the organization and the business.

The goals and the objectives of the MIS would be so stated the they can be measured.

The typical statements of the goals are as under.

- Provide online information on the stocks, markets and the accounts balances.

- The query processing should not exceed more than three seconds.

- The focus of the system will be on the end user computing and access facilities.

- Information support will be the first in the strategic areas of management such as marketing or service or technology.

Hardware and Software Plan

Giving due regard to the technical and operational feasibility, the economics of investment is worked out. Then the plan of procurement is made after selecting the hardware and software. One can take the phased approach of investment starting from the lower configuration of hardware going over to higher as development takes place. The process is to match the technical decision with the financial decision. The system development schedule is linked with the information requirement which in turn, is linked with the goals and objectives of the business.

The selection of the architecture, the approach to the information system development and the choice of hardware and software are the strategic decision in the design and development of the MIS in the organization. The organizations which do not care to take proper decisions in these areas suffer from over-investment, under-utilization and are not able to meet the critical information requirement.

It is important to note the following points:

1. The organization.s strategic plan should be the basis for the MIS strategic plan

2. The information system development schedule should match with the implementation schedule of the business plan.

3. The choice of information technology is a strategic business decision and not a financial decision.

ASCERTAINING THE CLASS OF INFORMATION

Ascertaining the information needs of the management for the business execution is a complex task. The complexity can be handled if the information is classified on the basis of its application and the user, which becomes the basis for the ascertainment.

The classification could be as shown. The design of the MIS should consider the class of information as a whole and provide suitable information system architecture to generate the information for various users in the organization. Let us now proceed to ascertain to the information needs of each class.

5.4 ORGANIZATIONAL INFORMATION

One can define the organizational information as a whole and provide suitable information system architecture to generate the information for various users in the organization. Such information can be determined by constructing a matrix of information versus as shown.

It can be observed from the table that the information entity is one, but its usages are different. For example, the employee attendance information would be used by the personnel

FUNCTIONAL OBJECTIVES

Each function has its own objectives which are derived out of the corporate goals.

For example, the overall business plan objectives give rise to the objectives for each business function. Some of the business plan objectives are given below based on which each function in the organization derives its objectives.

- The total sales per month is Rs 10 million.
- The finished goods inventory, not to exceed Rs 1 million.
- The outstanding more than six months not to exceed Rs 0.2 million.
- The capacity utilization should be minimum 85 per cent.
- The employee attendance per month should be 99 per cent.

The functional goals and objectives are necessary to achieve overall corporate achievements. Most of such goals and objectives are potentially achievable within the managerial and physical resources that the manager has at his disposal. It is, therefore, necessary to inform the manager on the achievements of these targets on a continuous basis.

In summary, the functional information would emanate from the work design and procedures, the managerial responsibility accounting, and with reference to the functional goals and objectives. It would be determined by studying the work design and procedures and the responsibility accounting, and with reference to the functional goals and objectives. It would be determined by studying the work design and procedures and the responsibility which the manager holds for the business performance. That information, which measures the business activity and evaluates the performance on the key target areas, is the functional information. The source of such information is the managers and their functional heads who together execute the business activity.

KNOWLEDGE INFORMATION

The knowledge information creates an awareness of those aspects of business where the manager is forced to think, decided and act. Such information shows the trend of the activity or a result against the time scale.

For example, whether the sales are declining and the trend is likely to continue in the next quarter. The product is failing continuously on one aspect and the reason of failure is the process of manufacturing. Such information pin-points the area or entity and forces the manager to act. It highlights the deviations from the norm or standard and also any abnormal development which are not in congruence with the forecasts or expectations. Such information gives rise to business decisions, which will affect the process of business significantly. In some situations the strategic decisions may be necessary to solve the problem.

The knowledge information may cut across the functional boundaries of the organization. The action or decision may fall in other functional areas of business operations. The decision may fall in the domain of top management or the middle management. The knowledge information is required by the middle and top management as they are the ones who have conceived, planned and implemented the business plan. Hence, the knowledge information supports the functions of the middle and the top management. Knowledge information is tracked continuously and reported in a fixed format, for consistency and at fixed intervals for updating the knowledge base. The nature of this information is analytical and relates to the past,

DECISION SUPPORT INFORMATION

Most of the information required by the middle and the top management is for decision making. The information does not act as a direct input to the decision making procedure or formula but supports the manager in the efforts of decision marking. Information is used in a decision support system for model building and problem solving. The support may act in two ways, in two ways, one for justifying the need of a decision, and the other as an aid to decision making.

For example, the information on the non-moving inventory justifies the decision of its disposal at throwaway prices. The demand forecasts information aids in the decision on determining the economic order quantity for production or a sale. The decision support information can be determined for the company at the entity level leaving its use to the decision makers in a suitable manner. The source of this information could be internal or external to the organization. It can be determined by identifying the tools, techniques, models and procedures, used by the managers in the decision making.

OPERATIONAL INFORMATION

This information is required by the operational and the lower level of the management. The main purpose of this information is fact finding and taking such actions or decisions which will affect the operations at a micro level. The decisions may be to stay on overtime, draw additional material, change the job from one machine to the other, and send a reminder to the supplier for the supply of material.

These decisions are such that they make the routine administration of the business smooth and efficient. These decisions do not fall in the category of the managerial decisions.

The sources of operational information are largely internal through transaction processing and the information relates to a small time span and is mostly current.

DETERMNING THE INFORMATION REQUIREMENT

The sole purpose of the MIS is to produce such information which will reduce uncertainty in a given situation. The moment what is unknown becomes known, the decision maker.s problem simple. Methods have been evolved to handle the degree of uncertainty the management is expected to deal with.

An information system should meet the needs of the host organization it serves. The requirements for the information system are thus determined by the characteristics and procedures of the organizational system. But correct and complete information requirements are frequently very difficult to obtain. Simply asking prospective users of the information systems to specify the requirements will not suffice in a large percentage of cases. There are three major reasons for the difficulty in obtaining a correct and complete set of requirements The sole purpose of the MIS is to produce such information which will reduce uncertainty in a given situation. The moment what is unknown becomes known, the decision maker.s problem simple. Methods have been evolved to handle the degree of uncertainty the management is expected to deal with.

The difficulty to determine a correct and complete set of information is on account of the factors given below:

1. The capability constraint of the human being as an information processor, a problem solver and a decision maker.

2. The nature and the variety of information.

3. Reluctance of decision makers to spell out the information for the political and the behavioral reasons.

4. The ability of the decision makers to specify the information.

5. In spite of these difficulties, methods are evolved based on the uncertainty scale, starting from the low to the high level of

175

uncertainty. If the uncertainty is low, seeking information requirement or needs is easy as against a very high level of uncertainty.

5.5 METHODS OF HANDING UNCERTAINTY

Leval of uncertainty Level of management Method Low (Near certainty) Precise probabilistic knowledge (A risk situation) Not able to determine in probabilistic terms precisely (Very risky)

High (Total uncertainty)

Operations management.

Middle management

Middle and top management.

Top management.

There are four methods of determining the information requirements. They are:

1. Asking or interviewing

2. Determining from the existing system

3. Analysing the critical success factors

4. Experimentation and modeling.

5.6 DEVELOPMENT AND IMPLEMENTATION OF THE MIS

Having made the plan of the MIS, the development of the MIS calls for determining the strategy of development. As discussed earlier the plan consists of various systems and subsystems. The development strategy determines where to begin and in what sequence the development can take place with the sole objective of assuring the information support.

The choice of the system or the subsystem depends on its position in the total MIS plan, the size of the system, the user understands of the system and the complexity and its interface with other systems. The designer first develops systems independently and starts integrating them with other systems, enlarging the system scope and meeting the varying information needs.

Determining the position of the system in the MIS is easy. The real problem is the degree of structure, and formalization in the system and procedures which determine the timing and duration of development of the system. Higher the degree of structuredness and formalization, greater is the stabilization of the rules, the procedures, decision making and the understanding of the overall business activity. Here, it is observed that the user.s and the designer.s interaction is smooth, and each others needs are clearly understood and respected mutually. The development becomes approach with certainty in inputs process and outputs.

PROTOTYPE APPROACH

When the system is complex, the development strategy is Prototyping of the system. Prototyping is a process of progressively ascertaining the information needs, developing methodology, trying it out on a smaller scale with respect to the data and the complexity, ensuring that it satisfies the needs of the users, and assess the problems of development and implementation.

This process, therefore, identifies the problem areas, inadequacies in the prototype vis-à- vis fulfillment of the information needs. The designer then takes steps to remove the inadequacies. This may call upon changing the prototype of the system, questioning the information needs, streamlining the operational systems and procedures and more user interaction. A typical process of the system development through prototyping is given in Fig 8.1

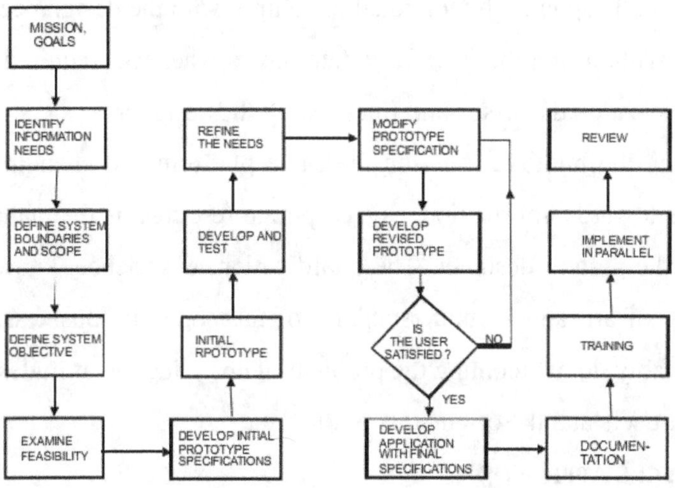

Fig. Information System Development Model; Prototyping Approach.

INFORMATION SYSTEM DEVELOPMENT MODEL; PROTTYPING APPROACH

In the prototyping approach, the designer.s task becomes difficult, when there are multiple users of the same system and the inputs they use are used by some other users well. For example, a lot of input data comes from the purchase department, which is used in accounts and inventory management.

The attitudes of the various users and their role as the originators of the data needs to be developed with a high degree of positivism. It requires, of all the personnel, to appreciate that the information is a corporate resource, and all have to contribute as per the designated role by the designer to fulfill the corporate information needs. When it comes to information the functional, the departmental, the personal boundaries do not exist.

These calls upon each individual to comply with the design needs and provide without fail the necessary data inputs whenever required as per the specification discussed and finalized by the designer.

Brining the multiple users on the same platform and changing their attitudes towards information, as a corporate resource, is the managerial task of the system designer. The qualification, experience, knowledge, the state of art, and an understanding of the corporate business, helps considerably, in overcoming the problem of changing the attitudes of the multiple users and the originators of the data.

Life Cycle Approach

There are many systems or subsystems in the MIS which have a life cycle, that is, they have birth and death. Their emergence may be a sudden or may be a part of the business need, and they are very much structured and rule-based. They have hundred per cent clarity of inputs and their sources, a definite set of outputs in terms of the contents and formats. These details more or less remain static from the day the system emerges and remains in that static mode for a long time. Minor modifications or changes do occur but they are not significant in terms of handling either by the designer or the users of the system. Such system, therefore, have a life and they can be developed in a systematic manner, and can be reviewed after a year or two, for significant modification, if any. Examples of such systems are pay roll, share accounting, basis financial accounting, finished goods accounting and dispatching, order processing, and so on.

These systems have a fairly long duration of survival and they contribute in a big way as sources of data to the Corporate MIS. Therefore, their role is important and needs to be designed from the view point as an interface to the Corporate MIS. The life cycle approach, therefore, has a method of its own as explained.

Apart from the core systems, some decision support systems can be developed through the life cycle approach. The choice of system design in the prototype and Life Cycle approach is decided on the basis of the nature of the system or application. For example, you have a choice of the database approach versus the conventional system approach, the online real time versus the batch processing approach. You may also have choice of hardware and software. All these technical decisions are more situation dependent, requiring judicious application of and information technology.

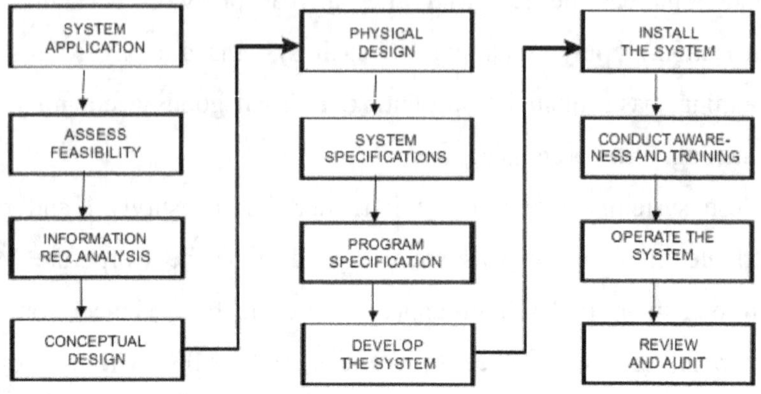

LIFE CYCLE APPROACH TO THE DEVELOPMENT OF MIS

Table 8.6 shows the difference between the two approaches helping the designer select an approach.

Table 8.6 Comparison of Approaches	
Prototyping approach	*Life cycle approach*
Open system with a high degree of uncertainty about the information needs.	Closed systems with little or no uncertainty about the information needs. The system remains valid for a long time with no significant change. The design would remain stable.
Necessary to try out the ideas, application and efficiency of the information as a decision support.	No need to try out the application of the information as it is already proven.
Necessary to control the cost of the design and development before the scope of the system and its application is fully determined. Experimentation is necessary.	Scope of the design and the application is fully determined with clarity and experimentation is not necessary.
User of the system wants to tryout the system before he commits the specification and the information requirements.	The user is confident and confirms the specifications and the information needs.
The system and application is highly custom oriented.	The system and application is universal and governed by the principles and practices.

5.7 COMPARISON OF APPROACHES

Prototyping approach Life cycle approach Open system with a high degree of uncertainty about the information needs.

Necessary to try out the ideas, application and efficiency of the information as a decision support. Necessary to control the cost of the design and development before the scope of the system and its application is fully determined. Experimentation is necessary.

User of the system wants to tryout the system before he commits the specification and the information requirements.

The system and application is highly custom oriented. Closed systems with little or no uncertainty about the information needs. The system remains valid for a long time with no significant change. The design would remain stable. No need to try out the application of the information as it is already proven.

Scope of the design and the application is fully determined with clarity and experimentation is not necessary.

The user is confident and confirms the specifications and the information needs.

The system and application is universal and governed by the principles and practices.

5.8 IMPLEMENTATION OF THE MANAGEMENT INFORMATION SYSTEM

The implementation of the system is a management process. It bring about organizational changes, it affects people and change their work style. The process evokes a behavior Response which could be either favorable or unfavorable depending upon the strategy of the system implementation.

In the process of implementation, the system designer acts as a change agent or a catalyst. For a successful implementation he has to handle the human factors carefully.

The user of the system has a certain fear complex when a certain cultural work change is occurring. The first system has foremost fear is about the security to the change-over form the old to new is not a smooth one. Care has to be taken to assure the user that such fears are baseless and the responsibility, therefore, rests with the designer.

The second fear is about the role played by the person in person in the organization and how the change affects him. On many occasions, the role may reduce his importance in the organization, the work design may make the new job impersonal, and a fear complex may get reinforced that the career prospects may be affected.

GUIDELINES

There are certain guidelines for the systems designer for successful implementation of the system. The system designer should;

1. Not question beyond a limit the information need of the user.

2. Not forget that his role is to offer a service and not to demand terms.

3. Remember that the system design is for the use of the user and it is not the designer.s prerogative to dictate the design features. In short, the designer should respect the demands of the user.

4. Not mix up technical needs with the information needs. He should try to develop suitable design with appropriate technology to meet the information needs. The designer should not recommend modifications of the needs, unless technically infeasible.

5. Impress upon the user the global nature of the system design which is required to meet the current and prospective information need.

6. Not challenge the application of the information in decision making. It is the sole right of the user to use the information the way he thinks proper.

7. Impress upon the user that the quality of information depends on the quality of input which he provides.

8. Impress upon the user that he is one of the users in the organization and that the information is a corporate resource and he is expected to contribute to the development of the MIS.

9. Ensure that the user makes commitment to all the requirements of the system design specifications. Ensure that he appreciates that his commitments contribute largely to the quality of the information and successful implementation of the system.

10. Ensure that the overall system effort has the management.s acceptance.

11. Enlist the user.s participation from time to time, so that he is emotionally involved in the process of development.

12. Realize that through serving the user, he is his best guide on the complex path of development.

13. Not expect perfect understanding and knowledge from the user as he may the user of a non-computerized system. Hence, the designer should be prepared to change the system specifications or even the design during the course of development.

14. Impress upon the user that the change, which is easily possible in manual system, is not that easy in the computer system as it calls for changes in the programs.

15. Impress upon the user that perfect information is non-existent; his role therefore still has an importance in the organization.

16. Ensure that the problems in the organization are resolved first before the system is taken for development.

17. Conduct a periodical user meeting on systems where you get the opportunity to know the ongoing difficulties of the users.

18. Train the user in computer appreciation and systems analysis as his perception of the computerized information system will fall short of the designer.s expectation.

Implementation of the MIS in an organization is a process where organizational transformation takes place. This change can occur in a number of ways.

The Lewin.s model suggests three steps in this process. The first step is *unfreezing* the organization to make the people more receptive and interested in the change. The second step is *Choosing* a course of action where the process begins and reaches the desired level, and the third step is *Refreezing*, where the change is consolidated and equilibrium is reinforced. Many a times, this process is implemented through an external change agent, such as a consultant, playing the role of a catalyst.

The significant problem in this task is the resistance to change. The resistance can occur due to three reasons, viz., the factors internal to the user of information, the factors inherent in the design of the system and the factors arising out of the interaction between the system and its users. The problem of resistance can be handled through education, persuasion, and participation. This itself can be achieved by improving the human factors, and providing incentives to the users, and eliminating the organizational problems before implementing the system.

5.9 MANAGEMENT OF QUALITY IN THE MIS INFORMATION EVALUATION AND QUALITY ASSURANCE
EXAMPLE CASE MANAGEMENT SERVICES

Substance abuse treatment programs, including those that receive public assistance, are increasingly operating in a managed care environment. Policymaking and clinical decision-making in a managed care environment depend on outcome data that have traditionally described the impact of case management and substance abuse treatment interventions in terms of services used and money spent. An additional demand for data comes from public and private payers who want services linked to specific outcomes.

In the past, public sector substance abuse programs were not paid to collect such data and were discouraged from using funds designated for service delivery to conduct evaluations. Consequently, evaluation services often were available only through demonstration grants or through the efforts of university-based evaluators. Today, however, many providers plan, fund, and perform their own evaluations. This reflects both the mandates of funding organizations and agencies' desire to refine or improve their services. To prepare treatment programs to get involved in these efforts, this chapter first presents findings from previous evaluation efforts and then proposes a framework for facilitating quality improvement and other evaluative efforts that consider multiple stakeholders and focus on myriad outcomes and data sources.

EVALUATING CASE MANAGEMENT PROGRAMS

In order for substance abuse programs to ascertain if case management works, the program and its various stakeholders (including funding and regulatory agencies) must specify and measure outcomes they regard as indicators of success.

In documenting a case management effort, it is important to start with *benchmarks* - expectations that are made concrete as measurable statements (e.g., "case managers spend 60 percent of their time in face-to-face contact with their clients"). Some of the sources that programs can use to establish benchmarks include

- Policy and procedure manuals

- Federal, State, and local case management standards

- Agency case management program descriptions and mission statements

- Literature on program models (if the program under evaluation is a replication)

- Consultants

The types of data required for an evaluation of case management, how the data are collected, and the manner in which data are put to use vary among different stakeholders. It is important to understand the types of data that various stakeholders need to evaluate the program. Structured feedback loops should be established to ensure that the data gathered are returned to various stakeholders in some meaningful way so that they have an impact on shaping future program development (and future data needs). One of the benefits of the case management approach is that it can be adapted to meet the sometimes contradictory needs of the various stakeholders.

Data needs of case managers

Although the data needs of case managers may vary from agency to agency, rapid access to data in three particular areas is critical:

- Information about clients currently on the caseload (roster management), including outcome data so case managers have feedback on their performance

- Data that allow case managers to track clients through various services

- Data that produce "flags" for follow-up letters, aftercare, and other time-sensitive functions

In addition to these elements, case managers with gatekeeping or budgeting responsibility need overall service utilization and cost figures by client in order to manage services within a budget. To evaluate process, case managers need access (preferably computerized) to referral networks, bed allocation systems, progress notes, and data related to the daily conduct of their jobs. In terms of outcome data, case managers may want rapid access to client status, especially if it would prompt additional efforts.

DATA NEEDS OF PROGRAM MANAGERS

Program managers must ensure that the data collected reflect the program mission and facilitate the program's management. While the case manager focuses on individual clients, the program manager analyzes data elements to see patterns and to flag and investigate "outliers" - those who deviate drastically from the statistical norms of the population.

The initial data needs of program managers reflect concerns with concrete aspects of program operation. To program managers, case management essentially begins when the phone rings, and therefore, their data needs are filled by asking the following basic questions:

- How many inquiries are we getting about services?
- Are we getting clients?
- From what area are our clients?
- Are clients entering care once they make contact?
- Are we responsive to clients' needs from first contact forward?
- Is the type of client changing?

In addition to collecting these initial data, program managers must be able to track clients through their services so they can decide how to alter service provision. Important questions include

- Who is in what level of care at what time?

- How does the service fit with their treatment plans?

- Is the program meeting clients' different cultural needs?

- Who is dropping out, and why?

- What service not currently provided is requested most frequently?

- How much money is being spent on a particular service?

Other questions relate to the program manager's administrative functions, including

- What are the case managers doing? What are their caseloads?

- What are the results of internal monitoring?

- Are we reaching the target populations?

- Are clients retained at the appropriate level of care?

DATA NEEDS OF COMMUNITY POLICYMAKERS

Community policymakers may be local government officials, members of community coalitions, representatives of local law enforcement agencies, school board members, or other interested community-based stakeholders. Since they are not often directly associated with treatment programs, they may not have a very sophisticated understanding of program goals and may think of outcomes in terms of questions like "Is the client sober or not?" or "Is there less crime?" They tend to be less interested in improved scores on standardized measures of client functioning than in easily defined and observable outcomes that affect the community, principally

- Taxes - Reducing costs to taxpayers in the areas of incarceration, unemployment, and welfare enrollment and reducing costs of case management and substance abuse treatment by substituting a costly treatment with a less expensive one

- Safety - Reducing neighborhood crime and the number of homeless persons loitering in business districts

- Social costs - Increasing the number of substance abusers who are working and improving care for children of substance abusers

DATA NEEDS OF DIRECTORS OF STATE ALCOHOL AND DRUG ABUSE AGENCIES

Directors of State substance abuse agencies value data elements that describe the overall accessibility, quality, and cost of the substance abuse treatment system. In addition, these directors require data to track and contain the growth of Medicaid and public sector behavioral health care expenditures, to put managed care systems in place, and to evaluate the effect of managed care (including the provision of case management) on the delivery of behavioral health care services.

Key data elements that State directors often want to see in evaluation efforts include

- Patterns of service utilization and costs, including the use of public hospital and residential treatment centers
- Numbers of clients working and withdrawing from welfare and Medicaid
- Numbers of clients avoiding prison, reducing child welfare cases and costs, and reducing food stamp usage
- Numbers of appeals and grievances by clients

- Number and characteristics of substance abuse patients accessing other publicly funded social services

Increasingly, State directors of substance abuse agencies are becoming less isolated and are beginning to look for opportunities to exchange data among previously independent departments (e.g., mental health departments, Medicaid offices, and criminal justice offices). Some State agencies share access to statewide data sets. In addition, the movement toward managed behavioral health care has prompted more integration of data between State Medicaid offices and State substance abuse and mental health authorities.

DATA NEEDS OF THIRD PARTY PAYERS

Third party payers such as insurance companies need data that justify case management as a cost above and beyond the direct costs of treatment services (see Chapter 6). In addition, when case management is used to coordinate care, third party payers want to know whether clients are receiving the right services, at the right level of care, and in the right sequence, and to ensure that clients who are no longer in need are no longer receiving services. To that end, important data elements include

- The severity of the client's illness
- Assignment to levels of care
- Patterns of service utilization
- Use of free self-help or volunteer organization services
- Urinalysis results, use of other drugs, and scores on standardized outcome indicators

- Discharge determinations

DATA NEEDS OF CLIENTS AND FAMILY MEMBERS

Clients and family members may serve on advisory or governing boards of local programs or may be involved in family or peer support groups within the community. They may use outcome data, especially results of client satisfaction surveys, to change programs and policies or to choose services and providers. They may be less interested in patterns of service utilization or standardized scores on outcome evaluations than in how the system functions from the user's perspective. In fact, clients might consider a program successful if it is supportive, reliable, and easily accessible, as opposed to "efficient."

Data elements important to clients and family members include

- The availability and accessibility of services
- The freedom of choice (of services and providers) that the system allows
- The use and effectiveness of the appeals and grievance process
- The influence of input from consumers and family members
- Effectiveness of treatment
- Acceptability of treatment among the targeted populations

Specifically, clients seek answers to the questions

- Am I getting the right services, in the right setting?
- Are there systems I can access myself?
- How appropriate is my care?

5.10 MANAGEMENT INFORMATION SYSTEMS

The management information system contains all this information and allows stakeholders to use it. Managed care has provided the behavioral health care field with an example of how to manage far-flung data on clients.

One evaluation task for local programs is determining how to use data already routinely collected by a statewide MIS or managed care company-based MIS, saving the program from duplicating primary data collection. Another important task is to develop or enhance program-level MIS that track data the program needs locally, integrate with other computer-based or paper-based systems, and supply data required by third party payer and governmental bodies. All staff members of a specific program should be stakeholders in the MIS, which increases both system accuracy and the likelihood that a broad array of staff members will use it. If an agency does not have the resources to develop a sophisticated system, it should be able to automate at least a minimum amount of client information through commercially available software.

Local programs that are part of a managed care network undoubtedly will be included in a larger MIS sponsored by the umbrella provider. Providers who are not part of these networks may need to assess their readiness to take on managed care activities by evaluating their current MIS capabilities. Today, it is critical that an MIS be designed with the data requirements of managed care organizations in mind. The following guidelines, adapted from a Federal technical assistance publication, may help a program determine whether its existing MIS is sophisticated enough to support managed care operations. A program's MIS will suffice if it does each of the following:

- Retrieves patient information online or in less than an hour
- Cross-matches client records, use of services, and financial and insurance information
- Permits individual inquiries from managed care organizations
- Produces information that is used by clinicians, supervisors, and managers
- Integrates information from other programs and sites
- Allows client and service information to be reported to all major payers
- Generates patient invoices.

An existing MIS that can perform all of the above functions will likely support managed care and program demands; if it cannot, the program needs to strengthen deficient areas. Changes and advancements in data collection and access to patient information must be accompanied by appropriate protections for client confidentiality.

5.11 FUTURE RESEARCH

Research focused on case management in the substance abuse field is limited and offers many opportunities for local substance abuse programs to make significant contributions to the field. Suggested directions for future research include the following:

- Key ingredients of successful programs, especially for hard-to-reach populations

- Relative cost-effectiveness of particular case management models, including cost outcome results within systems incorporating full parity of substance abuse with other health care, outcome results when a full continuum of care is available to patients, and outcome results associated with use of standardized guidelines for placement, continued stay, and discharge for substance abuse patients
- Improved methodology to investigate research questions in "real world" settings
- Development of brief versions of valid and reliable research outcome instrumentation
- The effect of particular forms of case management on societal costs of substance abuse and its treatment
- Cost shifting among health, behavioral health, criminal justice, and other systems that can be accessed by the target population
- Creative ways to use secondary data sets (such as Medicaid and Medicare) to determine trends and patterns of care
- Research questions from broader sociological or multi-disciplinary perspectives

EVALUTION

- As we develop different choices of information technology and its configurations, the decision making enters into the evaluation phase for selection. The selection criteria for evaluation would have different dimensions to be satisfied simultaneously. These dimensions are as follows:

1. Technical Evaluation

2. Operational Feasibility

3. Financial Consideration

TECHNICAL EVALUATION (TE)

Technical evolution deals with the testing parameters, such as data transfer needs, the response level, the successful connectivity of the different hardware platforms, and the degree of meeting the overall system performance standards.Technical evaluation can be carried out first by studying the literature of the product in detail and then by conducting brain storming sessions with the vendors specialists. In this phase a number of doubts are clarified and the vendors. claims in the areas of the system performance are confirmed. Technical evaluation can then be planned by scheduling the activities such as the bench marking for a couple of key parameters. The bench marking studies could be at a .raw. level where you test the vendors specifications. Once these are confirmed, the specifications are put to test on a live platform, i.e., the technical specification are tested by running live data in a particular format. Such an experiment would be a prototype model of your information processing need related to the mission critical applications. You may develop a mini representative processing application and run it on a model configuration of the system. Such experiment would confirm the vendors. claims and your expectations and needs. This would develop certain norms which can be used to configure the hardware details and building the architecture. The bill of material of hardware and software can be worked out with the help of these norms.

Following hardware software details are configured and the quality of each item is also decided using the norms developed in a live experiment.

The decisions on the following points would facilitate the system configuration for a given requirement.

- Memory and Cache
- Disk Capacity, Features, Controllers
- CPU Speed, Processing Architecture and Capabilities
- Servers
- Terminals-PCs, X Terminals Work Station
- Network and Cabling, Internet and Intranet
- EDI, E-Mail
- Network Hardware
- Output Devices
- Monitors
- Operating System
- Standard: ASCII, ANSI, GUI
- Hardware Architecture
- System Software: OS, Gateways, Interfaces, Drivers, Utilities and Compilers
- Media, Copying Devices
- RDBMS, FEATURES
- Packages

Technical evaluation and confirm the information technology approach to the information processing needs of the organization. The issues like the centralized versus distributed, hardware choices as all the vendors may not satisfy the requirement of the organization.

Having narrowed down the hardware configurations to two or three options, the technical evaluation considers the performance related issues such as reliability, dependability, performance on the volume scale, security, integrity and autonomy, etc. All the option may not equally satisfy the evaluation standards set by the organization on these factors. The performance related issues will help fine tune the configuration details such as the memory, the number of ports, the specific input and output devices and the hardware infrastructure. Technical evaluation also helps to break down the hardware on a time scale, i.e., the minimum required in the initial stage and subsequent add-ons, expansions and upgrades on a time scale. In technical evaluation we are discussing information technology. The information technology is constantly under development and the scale on which such improvement takes place is phenomenal. Hence, it is necessary to select the latest technology in all areas of information processing as it would take you a long way and help you to protect the investment. The investment is protected, if the Information Technology choice is scalable, upgradeable and also expandable with the growth of he online versus the batch versus the real time, the network versus the mini or the superman are also evaluated. Technical evaluation also helps in narrowing down the the business.

- The options approved after the technical evaluation are tested on the operational feasibility. What the technology offers may not be possible to operate at the practical level and scale to obtain full benefits of the various inherent features. The operational feasibility evaluation considers the people-related issues and whether the systems and the procedures of the organization are complementary and conducive.

- In a number of situations, the choice of technology determines automatically the caliber, the competence, and the knowledge of the people in the organization. It is also observed that the organization does not provide people support to implement technology successfully. The shortcomings on peoples. side would be the lack of requisite qualification and the subject knowledge, the ability to absorb the technology, and use it effectively. Many a times, the organization would require appointing a new set of personnel to fulfill these needs.

- Other areas affected would be the systems and the procedures currently operating in the company. The shortcoming is observed right from the absence to the inefficient systems and procedures. The modern information technology needs sophisticated back-up of the data at a requisite point and time. If such a data support is not available then the information technology would be underutilized or may not be worthwhile to implement.

- For example, the information technology offers a solution of fast data transfer and processing between the two platforms at two locations, i.e., the data source is at one location and its need is at two other locations. Due to the systems and the procedures prevailing at the source location, the arrival of the data at the required location is late and hence not useful. Hence, the information technology solution is operationally infeasible to obtain the best of the solution.

- Most of the issues in the operational feasibility evaluation are related to the people and business processes (system and procedure). The environment must support proper implementation of a new information technology.

- If the environment does not support the new technology, it will be managerially prudent to choose next best option by obtaining full benefits in its successful implementation and further at a later date to switch over to the original best option.

FINANCIAL EVALUATION

- All the option can be evaluated in terms of the invested it calls for. It is always possible to rank the option on the basis of the basis of the investment. All business investment is valuated in terms of return on the investment (ROI) or certain payback period. They are also judged from budget considerations.

- The information technology investments are difficult to judge on the ROI basis as some aspect of the investment are intangible and are difficult to quantity in monetary terms.

- The best approach in such cases is to judge the investment in terms of the value of information it gives on an incremental scale. If the value of information in relation to its investment is not significant, then it could be advisable the consider the next best lower investment option.

- In regard to the budget restrictions, it would be advisable to examine the possibility of scaling the hardware and the software options. It is then possible to have a solution implemented in terms of the budget provisions. The scaling can be done in terms of the quality of hardware required in the option.

- If may be possible to buy the requisite minimum in the first year and expand them in the subsequent period. It may be possible to configure the hardware in terms of the capabilities which are required now and which can be acquired later on. For example, one can start on 32MB memory and over to 64MB. One need not buy all the software in the first place. It can be phased out in terms of need, i.e., purchased the requisite software as and when required.

- The budget restrictions can handle by taking the benefit of the scalable and the upgradeable technology. The scaling of the expansion can be done on two scales, viz. horizontal and vertical expansion. The horizontal expansion relates to the quantity while the vertical expansion relates to the quality and coverage.

HORIZONTAL EXPANSION

- The memory, disk, terminals, peripheral equipment, etc. can be configured for the present needs and then expanded as the coverage increased.

VERTICAL EXPANSION

- The system integration, backward or forward, concentrates on the mission critical applications, covering only the main key business functionalities.

- However, in all these matters the total decision is to be taken first and then broken down into components and in terms of the budget provisions for the next two years or more.

- In all these matters, a thought should be given to protect the information technology investment. If certain technological advances are round the corner, then it is better to defer the investment. The choice of hardware and software should be such that it should facilitate the integration of new technology into the old one. The new version of upgrades should be independent of the hardware. The application languages should be such that any open system can absorb it without many changes. The software choices should be independent of the hardware configurations such as the LAN, the WAN, the MINI etc.

- Many a times, the packages cannot run on all the platforms because of the chip and the architecture of the hardware platform. The open system architecture is not always that .open. to accept all the software.

EVALUATION AND MONITORING

- A manager's effectiveness is largely dependent on the existence of an equally effective management information system *MIS*. An MIS provides information on a variety of different organizational functions, allowing a manager to plan, monitor, and evaluate operations and performance. MIS outputs also enable a manager to make strategic decisions and intelligent choices that shape an organization's future vision and mission.

- *Monitoring and evaluation* are 'twin sisters'. They assist management in knowing whether program objectives are being achieved, to what extent there is need for mid-course correction to address emerging problems, in the environment, or and assess employees' efficiency, and maintenance of standards. Both examine indicators, targets, criteria and standards. The meanings, and definitions of monitoring and evaluation are often contentious because of the two activities' substantial overlap.

5.12 CHOICE OF THE INFORMATION TECHNOLOGY AND THE MANAGEMENT INFORMATION SYSTEM

The choice of the information technology is a backbone of the Management Information System. It is a critical, strategic decision affecting the business operations and prospects. It affects the people, the processes and productivity and helps organization emerge with a new work culture. Since, it is a high investment decision; the management would look at it from the return it yields in the business.

The success of the MIS lies in how the information technology is implemented in the organization. A lot depends on the people and their ability to accept the new work style and the new work culture. All the implementation of the information technology leads to organizational transformation in the content and structure.

If the human face of the organization is not properly aligned to the information technology, the best information technology would fail in its implementation, adversely affecting effective development of the MIS. There is a risk in manipulating the information technology beyond a limit to suit the personnel of the organization or the budget limitation. Hence, the implementation of the information technology could be slow on the time scale to accommodate a certain critical constraint, but it should not be allowed to adversely influence the information technology decision itself.

The information technology changes are very rapid. To protect the investment in the information technology, the selection criteria should include features such as scalable architecture, upgradeable software, an open system environment, communication capability through gateways and interfaces and so on. A good management information system design requires a matching support from the information technology.

5.13 A System for Quality Assurance Has Been Institutionalized

DEFINITION:

Quality refers to offering a service or product in a way that consistently meets the clients needs. Quality assurance (QA) is a generic term describing a number of management approaches (Continuous Quality Improvement (CQI), Total Quality Management TQM)), all of which recognize that many organizational problems result from systems and processes, as well as from a lack of clear performance expectations, rather than negligence on the part of individuals. QA, as it applies to the management of reproductive health programs, generally involves the encouragement of staff members at all levels to analyze systems and processes, to use information to identify the nature and size of each problem, and to design and implement activities to improve services and client satisfaction. (For more detail on QA, see the Service Delivery - Quality of Care indicators.)

DATA REQUIREMENT(S):

Evidence of the availability of quality standards and protocols; budget allocation for QA activities; performance/provider reviews of adherence to standards; client satisfaction feedback on quality; staff feedback on involvement in quality initiatives.

DATA SOURCE(S):

Organizational documents including service delivery guidelines; interviews with managers, supervisors, and other staff at all levels;

budget; staff performance reviews; training curricula; client satisfaction surveys; suggestion boxes.

PURPOSE:

This indicator measures organizational commitment to QA; more detailed indicators can be found in "Managing Quality and Clinical Services".

From a management perspective, the following six items are essential to developing a composite score of commitment to QA:

- **Evidence of integration of quality assurance into the organization's mission and strategy**

By measuring this item, an evaluator will first understand if an environment or Organizational culture of quality improvement exists.

- **Evidence of integration of quality assurance into the organization's plans and budget**

Not all QA activities will require a separate line item budget; some of them are combined with other activities and are done only at marginal cost. Assessment of budget allocation can be difficult unless the budget is highly detailed/annotated.

- **Evidence of the availability of quality standards or protocols.**

This indicator is easy to measure but requires identification of protocols for service delivery (clinical protocols, counseling) as well as for management (e.g., supervision, storage of supplies, infection prevention, MIS reporting) for each major type of reproductive health service.

- **Performance/provider review of adherence to standards.**

As with the previous item, this aspect requires measurement according to service delivery and management standards for each reproductive health area. It requires direct observation of staff (such as by a supervisor or mystery client); measurement can therefore be time consuming depending on the volume of services at a given facility.

- **Mechanisms for obtaining client satisfaction/ feedback on quality.**

Measuring client satisfaction is the principal means of knowing whether QA initiatives are reaping any benefits. Among the numerous methodologies for measurement, the most common is the client exit interview. One of the weaknesses of exit interviews is that clients sometimes forget details of a visit or do not know what practices are acceptable. Clients may fear impact of negative responses on availability of and access to services.

- **Mechanisms for collecting provider perspectives on quality.**

Measurement in this area can reveal gaps between client and provider understandings of quality. It can also help managers understand the extent to which providers feel encouraged or rewarded for taking initiative to address quality.

REFERENCES

1. "Management Information Systems (MIS)". Inc.com. Retrieved 10 March 2014.

2. "Social Funds - Management Information Systems". The World Bank. Retrieved 5 March 2014.

3. "Types of Information Systems". UNC Charlotte. Retrieved 5 March 2014.

4. Alonso, S., Herrera-Viedma, E., Chiclana, F., & Herrera, F. (2010). A web based consensus support system for group decision making problems and incomplete preferences. Information Sciences, 180(23), 1 December. 4477-4495.

5. Awad, E. M., & Gotterer, M. H. (1992). *Database management.* Danvers, MA: Boyd & Fraser.

6. Banerjee, U. K., & Sachdeva, R. K. (1995). *Management information system: A new frame work.* New Delhi: Vikas Publishing House.

7. Bidgoli, Hossein, (2004). The Internet Encyclopedia, Volume 1, John Wiley & Sons, Inc. p. 707.

8. Certo, S, C. (1997). Modern Management, diversity, quality, ethics and the global environment, 7th Ed, New Jersey, Prentice-Hall Inc. Davis, G.B., & Olson, M.H. (1985). Management Information Systems, conceptual foundation, structure and development, 2nd. New York, McGraw-Hill.

9. Davis, G.B., & Olson, M. H. (1985). *Management information systems: Conceptual foundations, structure, and development*. New York: McGraw-Hill.

10. Gordon, J.R. (1993). A diagnostic approach to organizational behavior, 4th Ed, New York, Prentice-Hall Inc, Englewood Cliffs, NJ.

11. Gorry, G. A., & Michael M.M.S. (1971). A. Framework for Management Information System. Sloan, Management Review, 13 (Fall), 55-70

12. http://www.occ.gov/publications/publications-by-type/comptrollers-handbook/mis.pdf

13. Imboden, N. (1980). *Managing information for rural development projects*. Paris: Organization for Economic Co-operation and Development.

14. Joshi, Girdhar (2013). *Management Information Systems*. New Delhi: Oxford University Press. p. 328.ISBN 9780198080992.

15. Keen, P. G. W., & Morton, M. S. S. (1978). *Decision support systems*. Reading, MA: Addison-Wesley.

16. Laudon, K.,&Laudon, J. (2010). Management information systems: Managing the digital firm. (11th ed.). Upper Saddle River, NJ: Pearson Prentice Hall.

17. Laudon, Kenneth C.; Laudon, Jane P. (2009). *Management Information Systems: Managing the Digital Firm* (11 ed.). Prentice Hall/CourseSmart. p. 164.

18.Lucas, H. C., Jr. (1990). *Information systems concepts for management*. New York: McGraw-Hill.

19.Lucey, Terry (2005). *Management Information Systems*. London: Thomson. p. 336. ISBN 978-1-84480-126-8.

20.Lynn, Samara. "What is CRM?". PC Mag. Retrieved 5 March 2014.

21.Martin, J. (1990). *Telecommunications and the computer* (3rd ed.). Englewood Cliffs, NJ: Prentice-Hall.

22.Mason, R. D., & Swanson, B. E. (1981). *Measurements for management decision*. Reading, MA: Addison-Wesley.

23.McLeod, R., Jr. (1995). *Management information systems: A study of computer-based information systems* (6th ed.). New Delhi: Prentice Hall of India.

24.O'Brien, J (1999). *Management Information Systems – Managing Information Technology in the Internetworked Enterprise*. Boston: Irwin McGraw-Hill. ISBN 0-07-112373-3.

25.Pant, S., Hsu, C., (1995), Strategic Information Systems Planning: A Review, Information Resources Management Association International Conference, May 21–24, Atlanta.

26.Power, D. J. (2002). Decision Support Systems: Concepts and Resources for Managers. Editor, DSSResources.COM. Quorum Books division, Greenwood Publishing.

27.Published by Canadian Center of Science and Education 169 Simon, H. (1997). Administrative Behavior: A Study of Decision-Making Processes in Administrative Organizations, 4th Ed. The

Free Press. Stair, R.M. (1992). Principles of Information Systems: A Managerial Approach. Boston: Boyd and Fraser Ahituv, N., Neumann, S., & Riley, H. N. (1994). *Principles of information systems for management* (4th ed.). Dubuque, IA: Wm. C. Brown Communications.

28. Published by Canadian Center of Science and Education 169 Simon, H. (1997). Administrative Behavior: A Study of Decision-Making Processes in Administrative Organizations, 4th Ed. The Free Press. Stair, R.M. (1992). Principles of Information Systems: A Managerial Approach. Boston: Boyd and Fraser Ahituv, N., Neumann, S., & Riley, H. N. (1994). *Principles of information systems for management* (4th ed.). Dubuque, IA: Wm. C. Brown Communications.

29. Raheja, S. K., & Jai Krishna (1991). *Manual for monitoring and evaluation of T & V agricultural extension system.* New Delhi: Centre for Agricultural and Rural Development Studies.

30. Ramesh Babu, A., & Singh, Y. P. (1987). Management information system in an agricultural extension organization. In *Proceedings of the national seminar on management of information system in management of agricultural extension* (p. 1-15). Hyderabad: NIRD.

31. Ramesh Babu, A., & Singh, Y. P. (1990). Agricultural administration at block level: A case study. *Indian Journal of Extension Education, 26* (1 & 2), 88-90.

32. Rao, C. S. S. (1985). Agricultural extension management system in India: Past, present and modalities in future. *Indian Journal of Extension Education, 21* (1 & 2), 32-35.

33. Raymond McLeod, Jr. (1998). Management Information Systems, 6th Ed. New Jersey: Prentice Hall.

34. Raymond, McLeod, Jr. (1990). Raymond, Information Systems. New York, Macmillan Publishing Company. www.ccsenet.org/ijbm International Journal of Business and Management Vol. 6, No. 7; July 2011

35. Russell, H. M. (1979). A review of management information systems for agriculture. In H. M. Russell (Ed.), *Information for agriculture: Proceedings of the national workshop on agricultural information* (p. 41-51). Melbourne: Department of Agriculture, Victoria.

36. Sachdeva, R. K. (1990). *Management handbook of computer usage.* Oxford: NCC Blackwell.

37. Sanders, D. H. (1988). *Computers today* (3rd ed.). New York: McGraw-Hill.

38. Simon, H. A. (1977). The new science of management decision. New Jersey: Prentice-Hall.

39. Singh, Y. P., & Ramesh Babu, A. (1985). Basic management issues in extension. *Indian Journal of Extension Education, 27* (1 & 2), 20-31.

40. Taylor, Victoria. "Supply Chain Management: The Next Big Thing?". *Sept. 12, 2011*. Business Week. Retrieved 5 March 2014.

41. *Transaction processing systems (TPS)* collect and record the routine transactions of an organization. Examples of such systems are sales order entry, hotel reservations, payroll, employee record keeping, and shipping.

42. Wentling, T. L., & Wentling, R. M. (1993). *Introduction to microcomputer technologies. Rome: FAO.*

43. *Wikipedia.org.searchdatacenter.techtarget.com/definition/MIS*

44. *www.ccsenet.org*

45. *www.citesearx.ist.psu.edu.journal-archieves28.webs.com*

46. *www.cpu.unc.edu*

47. *www.ncbi.nntm.gov*

48. *www.openlearningworld.com*

49. *www.pathfinder.org*